This Book SHREDS

Learn How Music Can Help You Live With Purpose, Make Friends, and Create Magical Moments

BY ROB SPAMPINATO

This Book Shreds: Learn How Music Can Help You
Live With Purpose, Make Friends, and Create Magical
Moments
Copyright © 2022 Rob's School of Music
by Rob Spampinato

Cover artwork by: Kristin N. Spencer & Travis Spencer

ISBN-13: 978-1-957817-00-2

ISBN-10: 1-957817-00-3

On the web: robsschoolofmusic.com

Contact the author:
rob@robsschoolofmusic.com

This book is dedicated to my son, Jack.

"I'll give you all that I have in life.
I will protect you from the coming of
life's hard times.
You'll never cry, you'll never fall,
Never feel despair alone.
I am here forever, your home."
–Lyrics from "Legacy", written when I
found out I was going to be a dad.

Table of Contents

CHAPTER 1

When the Music Starts

"This is your time to finally allow yourself to learn, to make mistakes, and to become the version of yourself—not anybody else—that you want to be."

–Rob Spampinato

Have you ever looked at a musician up on stage, the lights dancing around them, the audience singing every lyric, and wondered, "Why can't I be like them?" Music is powerful. The connections and experiences we make through listening to and dancing to music as we journey through life are unparalleled. Songs that played during vital moments of the past always cause memories to come rushing back to us.

Whenever I hear Metallica's "For Whom the Bell Tolls," an instant transformation takes place. I'm 13 again, hanging out with my best friends, Brian and James, staying up all night in a room packed with albums and concert bootlegs and the promise of an unknown future.

I'm learning to play my first song on the guitar, ever. It's a magic bullet. We're eating Entenmann's chocolate-glazed donuts and drinking Pepsi. Even though I've just gotten serious about the guitar, I already know how to press the strings and wield the pick to extract the song, one note at time.

I feel the love for all of it swelling in my chest and bursting out as I scream the lyrics while I play. Even back then, I knew that music was my purpose. No matter what else happened, I was going to figure out a way to make music part of my everyday life.

Fast forward a few years, or decades—whatever— and you'll find me in Rob's School of Music, where I make music part of my students' everyday lives, still one note at a time. And when they come to me, thinking of the last live performance they saw, and asking "Why can't I be like them?" I know how I'll answer. In this book, I'm going to answer that question for you as well.

One of the most important lessons I've learned as a professional guitarist over the last 26 years is that it's never too late to turn your dream into reality. With my music students, I get to witness the truth of that fact every minute of every day. I can't tell you how many people have come in, or logged on to a digital class, and said this to me: "Rob, I love music, but I just never learned what I needed, and now I'm afraid it's too late." Whether the student is 10 or 75, they worry that they didn't start young enough. But it's never too late to learn how to rock. And it's never too late to experience the magic in the machine that music wants to bring into your life.

WHO NEEDS THIS BOOK?

The reason I wanted to write all the things I share with students down is because I realize now, after years of working with discouraged could-be musicians, that there are just too many hearts out there waiting to be filled up note by note. If you've ever had the longing deep down in your soul to pick up a guitar, a microphone, or a pair of drum sticks, you know exactly what I mean.

There are so many creative souls who would benefit from music in countless ways, but the world presses them down. If you've always wanted to learn an instrument, but haven't, it's not your fault. Just think about all the voices around you that say, "Why would you ever do that? What? Do you think you're going to be the next Bon Jovi or Taylor Swift?"

I know that trying something new is scary. If it wasn't, I would have a million new students pouring into my school every day. Because who doesn't want to make music? But you don't have to be afraid. One of the best lessons music teaches us is that it's okay to make mistakes. Anytime you face something unfamiliar, your brain will tell you to resist. It will throw up every alarm you have. But music won't hurt you.

If you approach it the way I'm going to teach you to in this book, music can only bring positive things into your life. No one ever picked up a guitar to have a bad time, right? And you won't have a bad time, either.

So, have you heard the call? Does your soul cry out for metal or jazz or classical music? Then this book is for you. And with my help, you're finally going to answer your heart's cry to allow music to transform your life.

WHO IS ROB SPAMPINATO?

Hi, my name is Rob. I've been obsessed with music for the last 27 years, but it didn't start out that way. Have you ever read a comic book or seen a comic-inspired movie? If yes, you know that every hero has an origin story. And my origin probably looks a little different than you would think.

It all started because of my dad, Al Spampinato. I love you, Dad. You see, my father is a professional drummer. And not just a guy you call for whatever. He's damn good. Growing up, there were always people playing music at my house. My dad even played and recorded with people I didn't realize were important in the music industry until much later, like Johnny Maestro & The Brooklyn Bridge.

When I seemed interested in the guitar, even

though I was only five, my dad took it seriously. He got me a little Stratocaster knock-off with a built-in amp by a company called Terminator. He also found me an instructor and I started lessons. Less than a year later I was miserable. The strings were still hurting my fingers and I wasn't really connecting to my teacher. I told my dad I wanted to quit, but I didn't expect what happened next.

My dad, my hero, the one who has always cheered me on, took my tiny Strat knock-off, and hurled it into the front yard. I still have the vivid image of the guitar turning and tumbling through the air before landing on the grass with a thud. At the time, I didn't understand why my dad was so upset. Looking back, I think it was because he knew what music could be for me. But he didn't give up. He let me quit, and then he waited for what probably felt to him like six long years.

I met James Mirarchi in karate class when I was almost 13 and James was 15 and something amazing happened. Even though I didn't know it then, he was about to transform my life, and we were about to embark on a quest built by friendship, grit, and a shared infatuation with Metallica. James loved music as much as my dad did, but unlike me, he didn't just want to listen to it: he wanted to make it. And he made me remember that I used to share that same dream.

Under James's influence, I picked up my still intact Strat knock-off and started strumming again. It wasn't long before my dad enthusiastically bought me a better guitar. That was the beginning of my lifelong obsession with music, but it almost didn't happen. Maybe you have a similar story. In fact, a lot of my students come in and have the same sorts of stories. It got me thinking. I had to answer the question: what made me want to give up on music?

Looking back, the only thing I uncovered was that my teacher made music miserable for me. He didn't try to connect with me in a way that would help me understand how to play music. He ran me through the same exercises and lessons he took everyone else through. But I was five, and I needed a different approach. And now, whenever I have a five-year-old kid as a student, I work five times as hard to make sure that they fall in love with playing on the first try.

What started out as a fun way to spend all my free time evolved until I started touring as a lead guitar player. I learned by trial of fire, and in this book, you're going to experience my musical journey as I walk you through eight important lessons I've learned over the last two decades. The reason I'm sharing these stories and lessons isn't to get you to sign up for music lessons at my school, though I'll be thrilled if you do. The real reason I want to tell you all of this is because I know what music has done for me, and I know it can do the same thing for you.

Isn't it time to finally go after the dreams you've always had? Isn't it past time to fill your heart up with all that music has to offer you? Don't wait another day. Join me as I take you through a story that can be yours, too, if you go after it.

WHY IS ROB THE MUSIC TEACHER YOU CAN TRUST?

A few paragraphs ago, I told you about my first music teacher: the one who didn't try to help me play the guitar in a way I could understand. Because of that, I have a customized approach to learning for each and every student that chooses my school.

I want you to know that it's okay to make mistakes: that's how you learn. I want you to know that music learning can be accessible, digestible, and approachable. A lot of people will tell you exactly what you should and shouldn't do when learning to play music, and that's intimidating. I don't operate that way. If you want to reach your goals, though, you need to be willing to challenge yourself. That's exactly what I'm going to teach you to do in this book. It's time to move past sitting down to play the same three songs you memorized forever ago. Why now?

If you don't start picking up your instrument, or using your vocal instrument now, today, the regret you'll feel will be super real. I've seen it too many times and I don't want that for you. Whenever I work with someone, after a few lessons, they always say the same thing: "Why didn't I do this sooner?" And if you want to know how fast you can learn an instrument, there's just one question you need to answer: How much are you going to practice?

It's time for me to draw back the curtains on the performance of my life to help you understand all the amazing tools music has been waiting to bring into your reality. Don't wait. Don't risk regret. Decide today that you're going to go on this journey with me so that you can finally go after what you really want. What you've always wanted: to make music a bigger piece of your soul.

SUMMARY

- Music is powerful. The connections and experiences we gain through music matter to us for the rest of our lives.
- Music is magic built into a machine. You can both play and experience it as a listener.
- It's never too late to make your dream come true (and that includes learning to shred on the guitar).
- Music is beneficial even if you never become the next Bon Jovi or Taylor Swift.
- Trying something new is scary, but learning music won't hurt you.
- Rob is obsessed with all things music.
- Musical friends are lifelong friends.

- Teachers who adapt to your unique learning style and age will help you succeed. Cookie-cutter instructions won't help you grow.
- How fast you shred, play, or sing is directly related to how much you choose to practice.

DISCUSSION QUESTIONS
1. Why do you want to play music?
2. In what ways can learning to play music enhance your life?
3. Do you have to stay scared, or can you move forward in the face of fear?
4. Is it ever too late to turn your dreams of learning to play music into your reality?

ROB'S MUSIC NOTES

When I thought of writing this book, I wanted to give you more than just my story. I know what it's like to feel that pull toward music, but not be able to implement basic things. I see my students struggle with this fact every day. So what I'd like to do is give you a bit of a music toolkit as you go through the book. You might be wondering, "How are you going to do that, Rob?" Great question. Let me tell you.

In each chapter, you are going to find a section called "Rob's Music Notes" where we go over different important ideas that shape the way we interact with music. In one chapter, you'll find a songwriting lesson.

In another, you'll learn how no matter where you play on the guitar's fret-board, if you hit a note that isn't part of the scale you mean to play, you're only half a step away from getting back on track.

You'll also get cool tricks I use every day to help harness your rock and roll mindset to build confidence from the ground up while learning to set measurable goals. I'll also teach you how to create a successful self-care routine.

It used to be that if you were a rocker, you couldn't be into exercise, healthy eating, or positive mindset. Thankfully, that has changed. In order to be a great musician, you need to feel the music. You need to embody confidence so that when people listen to you, that confidence comes through in what you play. With this book, you'll be able to do just that.

Now let's dive into the most important thing you need to know about music: it's a community, not a solo endeavor.

CHAPTER 2

Plug In – Connection Is Everything

"It's all about your friendships. A friend of mine, who is a studio engineer, knew someone [huge in the industry] who needed an acoustic player and he recommended me. I went in and was working with the producer who is also the music director, and we were having a good time and I was cracking jokes. This music director told me 'Yo man, I love your playing and you're fun to hang out with. We'll keep calling you.' Now I've been working with them for nine years."

–Rod Castro, (*Rod has played guitar with Beyoncé, TLC, Bebe Rexha, Bootsy Collins, Natasha Bedingfield, Ellie Goulding and also played for shows like X Factor, America's Got Talent, Gene Simmons Family Jewels, & LA Ink*)

My interest in music was born from one of the most important relationships in my life: the one between me and my dad. Since I grew up around music, my dad being the professional drummer and entrepreneur he was and still is, I know that without relationships music simply doesn't matter. That may sound extreme, but there are a lot of different ways that music is built on community, and in this chapter, I'm going to prove that to you.

Before I get to that, let me ask you a question: what would it be like to pour your heart into writing a song that you know will bring people joy, and then never be able to share it with anyone? Music isn't just played; it's experienced.

Have you ever seen Mr. Holland's Opus? Maybe not. I'm dating myself here since it came out in 1995, but it's worth streaming, for sure. It's a movie about a dad who's a music director at a school because he was never able to make it as a famous musician. He loves music. It's not an overstatement to say that music is his life. In an ironic twist of fate, his only child, a son, is deaf. Because of this, there is a disconnect between the father and son that can only be bridged when the father realizes he can experience music with his son.

The dad turns the speakers so their fronts are against the floor. That way his son can feel the music through the vibrations. Even those in the hearing-impaired community still want to experience music. They just have to find an unconventional way to do so.

Music is not meant to be enjoyed forever in solitude. If you want to have a successful career in music, you need to be willing to join the community that makes the music industry possible. I didn't learn how to be part of the musical community through a book like this, though, because books like this didn't exist back then. I had to learn it by getting out there, being willing to take risks, and enlisting my friends and family to help. If it wasn't for those things, I wouldn't be where I am today. And I sure wouldn't be the director of a music school that is part of a movement to make music a lifestyle instead of a hobby.

So how did I start my epic journey into the world of rock? Well, it began with a few Metallica addicts and a rusting U-Haul truck.

BLacK RoseS
(YES, THAT'S HOW WE WROTE IT.)

Everyone starts somewhere. We need to be honest with ourselves and understand that it's good to be humble about where we come from. My start was a garage band with my good friends James Mirarchi on guitar, Tom Pisani on drums, and a guy named Brendon Drew who later left and was replaced by Drew Kelly on bass. I was 17 years old and the only one brave enough to take on being the front man so I performed as both lead singer and lead guitarist. Back then I didn't realize that my best singing voice wasn't the best (someone would finally tell me that what I was doing was more like screeching than singing much later). But hey, at least I had guts.

Our band was named after emotional angst, much

like any other teen band. Some girl named Rose had broken one of my bandmates' heart and to punish her, we immortalized the betrayal in epic fashion by naming the band BLacK RoseS.

Building our band from nothing taught me just how important community is. My dad, along with other people in our town, rallied around us as we decided to raise money to have our first CD pressed. I'm not 1,000 years old, but that's what we did back then. Spotify and Apple Music were distant visions in the future unknown. In the end, we came up with the insane plan to play and film a concert at our local Antrim Playhouse in Suffern, New York and charge $10 a ticket. But in order to pay for the venue and be able to press the CD, we also needed to raise money some other way too.

In an amazing show of support, we not only sold out the show, but we had the community involved in every way possible. First, we sold T-shirts that were sponsored by local businesses with their names on the back. I think we had like 30 businesses support us this way. Second, with the help of my dad, we figured out how to offer food at a concession stand to make money that way. A friend from school, who was into AV, helped us with the stage show. Another friend recorded it so we could send out the VHS tape of us all over the place. Yes, a physical tape to go alongside the physical CDs. Hey, being old can be cool, just like being young can. Retro and vintage are words for cool, old things, right?

But the best part, the thing I remember most vividly was getting ready to go on stage in front of all our friends, families, and neighbors. I had gone home to change after we finished setting up. As I walked through the crowd back to the dressing room where the rest of my bandmates waited, I was completely anonymous. Because no one realized I was with the band, I could feel the anticipation of everyone around me. Their love, support, and pure excitement was palpable: it was everywhere no matter where I was in the theater.

When I finally stepped on stage, I was so overcome with emotion I wanted to cry. I didn't cry though, because it was time to rock! That's what everyone had come to see us for. And that's what we did. It was during that night that I caught my very first moment of music-based magic, and that gave me the craving for more.

NEVER BE ALONE

In 2008, I had moved up to touring with another band called In Question. There was one song we played at every venue that people always came to talk to us about after the show. This song, titled "Never Be Alone", was always one I would dedicate to someone in the audience. And the way the song is written, it can literally apply to anyone.

The song's story talks about someone in love

with another person. Unfortunately, the object of the main character's affection keeps giving them all these reasons why they can't be together. As the song progresses, the main character is obviously refusing to move on because they hope that someday the other person will love them back.

Unrequited love is a universal theme in that most people experience this unfulfilled longing at least one time in their lives. But the song doesn't end there. In the final refrain, the lyrics shift from "I'll never be alone" to "I'll always be alone."

You see, the character singing says they've given a piece of their heart to the one who doesn't love them back. At the end of the song, the singer realizes that if they give away a piece of themselves to someone who doesn't intend to give anything back, they won't be full. They won't be able to love again and so they'll always be alone.

Music can act like the love interest in the song. If you give it everything and never leave room for anything else in your life, you won't be able to give yourself to any other pursuit, including human connection. It's important for you to realize now that not everyone can be John Mayer. Not every person can be the front runner in a hugely popular music ensemble or solo career.

The only way to make it in music so that it feeds your life instead of draining it is to focus on your relationships as well. There are people around you who want that real point of human connection. And some of them are also in the music world. If you aren't invested in building friendships with the people you work with and if you aren't interested in taking care of your relationship with yourself by establishing a good self-care routine, you will burn out. You will end up alone. That's not what I want for you, and I'm sure that isn't what you want for yourself either. So how do people avoid this possible music-related pitfall? Let's all learn together from lead guitarist Arianna Powell.

GO WHERE THE GIGS ARE & MEET THE PEOPLE THERE

One of the things I do to help my music school students fast-forward on through the song of their personal musical journey is to interview experienced musicians on my YouTube channel. In just one hour, my guests will give my students years' and sometimes decades' worth of wisdom. There is one interview in particular that stands out when I think about embracing the music community. Let me tell you why.

Arianna Powell can shred it on the guitar like any of the greats, but she had a hard time finding people who needed her rock prowess at first. Now she plays with artists like Olivia Rodrigo, Halsey, and the Black Eyed Peas. How did that happen for her? Through community.

Arianna lived in the Pittsburgh area and was

planning to use her music education to teach and play, until she had an epic realization. She was playing in smaller venues, and one in particular usually played Beyoncé concerts on the TVs that were on every wall of the place. She realized that Beyoncé had an all-woman band and thought it would be amazing to be part of something like that. So she examined what other women guitarists had done and tried to replicate that process. The biggest part of that was going where the gigs and opportunities were.

Like a lot of other aspiring artists, Arianna decided to move to a big city. But she didn't just move there and get a normal job, which is what a lot of people do. She got to work and made an active effort to meet people who could connect her with other people. She gigged with people in studio sessions and on stage, all while she built out her own community. Eventually those people would call for her to sub for them when they couldn't play.

That's how she got into the places where she eventually connected with bigger artists. That's how she got to the place where she could play live guitar on SNL with Dua Lipa: she made friends with people. She also worked super hard too, to learn how to play the guitar like a boss. But without those friendships, her career might never have exploded as big or as fast as it did.

Please don't underestimate how huge that is.

When you read Rod Castro's quote on the first page of this chapter (you read it right? If not, go back and read it, it's awesome) you probably didn't think that me using a quote about creating relationships would be tied to everything important in building your music career. That's how important authentic, empathetic connections are. And not just in music. In any business or any life venture that's worthwhile.

SUMMARY

- Relationships are vital in the music world.
- Music is a way we interact with each other, even if it's only listening to music together.
- Music can be a solitary experience, but it is much better as a collective experience.
- Community is everything. Don't forget to use your support team. For me, that team looked like my dad, James, Tom, Brendon, and Drew.
- Be brave and bold, and you never know what can happen.
- Love and support can go a long way.
- Sometimes strange ideas (like printing ads from local business on T-shirts) work! Be creative.
- Living your music dream is great, but don't forget to balance that out with a good self-care routine.
- Go where the gigs are, and make friends.
- To make good friends, you have to be a good friend. Be empathetic and authentic.

Discussion Questions

1. Is music better alone or with a support group?
2. Who are the people in your life who are on your support team? Write their names down and send them a note later to let them know how much you appreciate them.
3. What will happen if you let fear keep you from practicing and learning your instrument?
4. What will happen if you give into fear and quit?
5. Who can you call when you need encouragement to keep going?

Rob's Music Notes – Songwriting Lesson

In the last section of this chapter, I told you about a song called "Never Be Alone." Now I want to tell you how I wrote it, and how I use two failproof methods to write compelling lyrics that are both universal and relatable every time: even when what I'm writing about isn't based on fact.

When I have students who are progressing well, one of the next steps I always suggest is that they try to write a song. This combines your musical skill with your imagination and this power team means endless possibilities. This suggestion is always met with resistance. Why? People say, "I haven't experienced anything yet in life that's worth writing a song about." That statement isn't true no matter your age or background, and I can prove it.

Think about these questions. Have you ever had a pet you loved? Have you ever lost something that was important to you? It could be something as small and simple as a notebook. Have you ever been to a place that made you feel like you were lit up from the inside and you couldn't wait to go back? However you answered these questions, you've just accessed something important inside yourself: universal emotions.

The indisputable truth is that universal emotions connect all of us. This is why storytellers can make readers cry and laugh with a good book. This is why reality television has become as popular as it is. Every human feels certain emotions. People love, grieve, and rejoice about millions and probably even billions of things every single day. And now, you can use that knowledge to write a relatable song that creates a point of human connection between you, the writer, and your audience, the experiencer.

When I talked about "Never Be Alone" earlier, I didn't tell you my show routine for the song. Before playing it, no matter where I was, I would find a woman in the audience. I would call out to her, "What's your name?" and she would respond. "Hey, Ashley," I would say, "This song is for you." And as I'm singing the lyrics that can apply to anyone who has experienced unreturned love, I point at Ashley. I want to help her understand that if she's felt that way, she's not alone. And unlike the character in the song, she doesn't have to give part of herself away to someone who doesn't appreciate her.

I reach out for Ashley's hand and sing to her, and finally the song closes with the line, "I'll always be alone." Ashley's probably crying by now and every other person in the audience is living through the same emotion as the character in the song. They're looking at Ashely and thinking about how amazing she is and how she shouldn't let anyone treat her that way.

By now, you're probably thinking that I'm going to launch into a backstory about how this song was based on a real thing that happened to me or one of my friends. Well, it's not. This song is made up. There isn't really any person who didn't love me back that I pined after for years. There isn't a Rose behind the scenes this time.

The truth is, the song is about no one. I thought it up after a few friends and I were talking about love and how the person you love might not love you back. It was that simple. And when you go to write a song, it can be just as easy. And now that you know the truth, it's time for me to walk you step-by-step through a songwriting tutorial. Are you ready to learn how to punch people right in the feels? Let's do this.

WRITE AN EPIC SONG – PART 1

There are two ways you can approach writing an epic song. The first one is to write something based on universal emotions, like In Question's song "Never Be Alone." The second way is to tell a story through the song. One great song based on a story narrative is "The Way" by Fastball. Go listen to it, I promise you won't be sorry.

The ultimate storytelling song example is "Cat's in the Cradle" by Harry Chapin (you've probably heard the Cat Stevens version). This ballad is about the deteriorating relationship between a father and son, which most people can relate to. The father works too hard and never spends time with his son, and in the end the son sadly follows in that tradition by ignoring his aging father. It's a great example of songwriting gone right. But sometimes, you can find a unique magic by combining both universal emotions and storytelling.

Have you ever heard "Tears in Heaven" by Eric Clapton? Warning, it's a tear jerker. I've seen grown men weep while listening to this song. Why? Because it's a story that has universal emotion in it. So how is it combining emotion-based writing and storytelling? Well, it's a story based on a real tragedy that happened in Eric Clapton's life: Clapton's 4-year-old son, Connor, accidentally fell out of a hotel window to his death. For copyright reasons I can't include the lyrics of his song in the book, but please go listen to it. Ask yourself, "What does this make me feel?"

If you want an example that doesn't involve such a deep grief (I get it, grief is hard) then you can look at a more modern example of an artist who uses both universal emotions and storytelling in her songs: I'm talking about the living legend of songwriting— Taylor Swift. While Swift is famous for writing break-up songs based on real life, if you listen to her more recent work, you'll see that she's embarked on a journey of rich storytelling, and without the break-up narratives.

On her album Folklore, which came out in July of 2020, the song "the last great american dynasty" is focused on the historical figure Rebekah Harkness. Harkness owned Standard Oil and created the Harkness Ballet. In the song we learn all about Rebekah and the controversy she caused. The lyrics echo the voices of the old money gents and dames in that area of Rhode Island who pose an interesting question.

They want to know how things would have gone differently for the Standard Oil fortune if Rebekah had never married Bill Harkness. These naysayers call it "the last great American dynasty," which also ended up being the song's title. The feelings in the song resonate with anyone who has ever felt like they weren't allowed to be part of a club: a universal emotion.

At the end of the song, Swift goes one step further toward genius and reveals what inspired her to write it in the first place. The house Rebekah Harkness bought, called "Holiday House," was purchased by Swift, as she reveals in the lyrics. And Swift also has that similar feeling, wondering if the people around her think she's loud and doesn't fit in.

It's an epic story that draws two women together from different time periods, compares their emotional experiences, and invites the listener of the song to do the same. It also poses the question, "Is what other people think about you really all that important?" The answer that Swift seems to suggest for both herself and Harkness is "No, it's not. Be true to yourself."

The moral of this section is there is more than one way to write an amazing song. Think of universal emotions like loss, love, and joy. Think of a story you want to tell. Write a song about one of the two. If you're brave and want to inch toward genius, combine the two and make everyone cry. I believe in you!

WRITE AN EPIC SONG – PART 2

The most difficult thing about writing a song is actually getting started. Don't believe me? Just look at how much writers complain about how intimidating the blank page is. Musicians face the same problem. If that is the hardest part of writing songs, what should you do about it? Easy. Stop listening to all of the doubters in your head and start writing!

If you don't have anything on the page, you don't have anything to tweak or edit. It's that simple. Once you get past the first few lines, which you can totally do, you will be surprised at how easy it is to keep going. In fact, to prove how simple it is, I'm going to write the lyrics to a song live, right now, in this book.

At random, I had a friend send me a topic to write on. I'll show you my initial thoughts and then describe what happens as I write through the lyrics.

My friend challenged me to write about Napa Valley, in Northern California, which is great because I love it there. I may or may not have a tattoo about wine inked across my chest.

STEP #1: WRITE DOWN YOUR INITIAL THOUGHTS

The first step I take is to sit and think about the topic I'm interested in writing a song about. I'll grab a notebook and start writing words and phrases that remind me of the subject. In this case, it's a place. I note what the subject has to offer as far as experiences go. Think of this as a free write.

In my notebook I've written the following:
Taste, smell, the salty smell of the ocean on the way up the coast, vines, grapes, romance, high quality, amazing food, scenery, rolling hills, leaves of green, a wine glass, the popping sound of corks, swirling in the glass, walking through the rich dirt, holding hands, refreshing breezes, the feeling of being away from it all, a much needed rest, a dimly lit restaurant with

the most amazing smells and tastes, the crackle of the thick crust of sourdough bread.

Step #2: Dig Deeper and Borrow Thoughts from Other People

There are definitely enough sights, smells, tastes, and emotions to write about now, but I like to go one step further. Next, I research the subject and get ideas outside of the ones that live in my head. Sometimes in the first phase of note-taking, you'll skip over obvious ideas. This is why research comes in handy. You can see in the section above that I didn't think of writing "the Pacific Ocean" even though I mentioned its salty smell. It's always helpful to get outside perspectives when you're writing a song, and the internet makes that easier than ever.

I write "Research" under my initial ideas, and then record more words and phrases:
Tasting notes (dual meaning, notes of taste in the wine, notes in the song), buildings in the local missions (white smooth plaster, hand-hewn beams, orange tiled roofs, a cross on the roof), 1779 (the year when the vineyards were replanted), The Pacific Ocean, Sonoma County, acres of land, cellars, casks, drips, legs (of wine), Josephine (the first female grower, vintner, and winery owner in Napa).

At some point, when I have twenty to forty lines full of notes, I know it's time to stop researching. I think I've found my story, and I want to feature Josephine as some part of it. You have to be careful about research, because it's something you can justify spending time on when you're too scared to actually start writing. You don't have to be scared. You've got me and we've got this.

STEP #3: START WRITING, NO PROCRASTINATION

The first time you try to write something, it might be crap. Honestly, the first lyric that jumped into my head was, "Standing there, that Josephine, skirts so long and vines so lean." I'm pretty sure that's crap, but that's okay, I'm just getting started. By the time I've finished a song, I usually have a sheet of notebook paper that is one-part readable lyrics, one-part lyrics I've aggressively scratched out. It's all part of the process. Time to try again.

The tasting notes tell centuries' story,
Rolling hills and tales of glory.
Bleeding purple, white, and red,
The bursting fruit, the skin it's shed.

I wonder what Josephine would say
if she could see it now.

I wonder what Josephine would say
if she could see it now.

Crashing waves lead to the sky,
Above the hills the birds will cry,
The tasting notes never run dry,
Corks pop joyful sounds in reply.

I wonder what Josephine would say
if she could see it now.
I wonder what Josephine would say
if she could see it now.

A sigh escapes, I feel refreshed,
The missions all around are blessed,
My appetite has been aroused,
Where cheese only comes from happy cows.

(I'll probably take the line out about the happy cows,
which is a reference to a California ad about dairy from
the state, but it actually made me laugh out loud when
I wrote it, so I left it in for you to see. Songwriting can
be fun, too! Don't think it's all super serious.)

The crackle of the crust of bread,
Leaves sourdough tasting notes in my head,
Tomorrow I will leave with dread,
This place where my heart lives part-time.

I wonder what Josephine would say
To the fact that often say away.
I wonder what Josephine would say
If she could see me now.

STEP #4: LEAVE YOUR LYRICS ALONE FOR AT LEAST 24 HOURS

Before you edit your song to death, leave it. Oftentimes, you'll find that you get better ideas after you walk away from your notepad. That's fine because that's what smartphones are for. I can't tell you how many lyrics or song ideas I constantly type into that thing. You have to promise me you won't edit the lyrics in your notepad for at least 24 hours. Let the words sit there. Think about the mood and tone of the song and decide if they match what you've written. Then after you've taken your mandatory break, go back and tweak things.

For example, I would probably change the third verse to:
A sigh escapes, I feel refreshed,
The missions all around are blessed,
My appetite cries out,
Rich soil grows food that's not without.

A Note on Rhyme Scheme:

As you can see, I have employed almost every kind of rhyme scheme in this song, including the scheme of no rhyme. You don't need to use some fancy poetic formula to write words that have meaning. Take the listener to a place or make them feel an emotion. And if you choose to rhyme, don't forget that rhyming dictionaries make life a lot easier.

Now, don't you feel like you too can write an amazing song? If I can, you can. Just remember that you can't edit anything on a blank page.

What About the Music?

Like I said before, there are three different approaches to songwriting when it comes to the process of creating both music and lyrics. Some people prefer to write the lyrics first. Others prefer to come up with the music, figure out the melody, and then write the lyrics. There is a third, rare group of people who do both at the same time. There is no wrong order to do this in, I promise, but you won't know which group your fit into unless you try.

I'm part of the second group. First, I come up with the music, record a melody of nonsensical gibberish into my microphone, and then sit down to turn those sounds into words that tell the listener something.

You can try out each way to test which process feels right for you. Just make sure you actually write! Don't get bogged down by the process. You can do this. I believe in you!

CHAPTER 3

From the First Note - Decide You Won't Quit Before You Start

"[One time] I was flying from New York, and ended up getting what's called a splenic infarction. So basically my spleen blew up on this plane. I blacked out and ended up in the ER, and you know, it was like one of those near-death experiences. In my mind I basically said, 'You know, life is short. Things can happen at any time. You never know if you're going to live 5 minutes or 50 years.' I took that upon myself and said, 'I'm going to go for this music thing.' You might as well spend your life doing the thing you're really, really, really passionate about."

–Rosh Roslin (*Rosh has played and worked with Def Leppard, Maroon 5, Melissa Etheridge, Andy Grammer, Steve Vai, A Perfect Circle, & Bush*)

One of the only things you can really control in life is whether or not you quit. You can't control the weather. You can't control what happens after that job interview. You can't control whether or not your spleen randomly explodes on an airplane. But you can control what you do. When it comes to music, this means you are the only one who gets to decide if you'll keep growing and learning, or if you're going to complain about your fingers hurting to your dad and watch him throw your guitar out onto the front lawn.

In this chapter, we're going to talk about how to choose inspiration over intimidation so that you don't convince yourself to quit before you've really given learning an instrument a chance. I want to preface what I'm about to say with this: if you sing, your instrument is your voice. Never forget that.

A lot of young musicians get tripped up with social media musicians, especially guitar players. They look at what they see on the screen. They listen to what they hear come through the speakers on their computer. Then, in dramatic fashion, they hurl their guitar into the dumpster outside their house. Just kidding, almost.

When I was growing up, we had guitar magazines. That was it. There weren't any videos of kid prodigies or doctored reels of people playing at twice the speed they can really play. We read articles. That was it. Everything else was in our imagination.

We didn't have hundreds, thousands, or millions of ways to compare ourselves to other players all day every day. The only person we could regularly compare ourselves to was our past selves. There is something powerful about realizing that the only person you should ever be comparing yourself to is your past self.

Now, if you want to play guitar, you can put videos

out there of yourself for others to see. But you can also see some kid playing guitar and think, "I'll never, ever be able to do that." In that important moment, you have a vital choice to make.

INTIMIDATION VS INSPIRATION

When you see something that makes you feel like you have a long way to go in your playing proficiency, you can either be intimidated or inspired. But I'll tell you right now, intimidation is pointless. You will never be that person, and that's a good thing. Listen, I know that I can never be Eddie Van Halen, because I'm Rob. And that's okay. You are you, and they are them. That's good. Otherwise, life would be super boring. In the film Wayne's World, why do Garth and Wayne run into trouble when they try to play "Stairway to Heaven" in their local guitar shop? Because the guys working there are sick of hearing it. (If you're too young to get this reference, feel free to Google it.) Even something as amazing as "Stairway..." can become annoying and boring if everyone chooses to play only that.

When you choose inspiration over intimidation, you look at musicians' videos differently. Instead of thinking "I'll never be that good," your thought becomes "They've found their thing, and that's awesome, and I can also find mine."

Some of the videos I see out there are doctored, and the expectation to be able to play like that is impossible. You need to understand that. What you also need to understand, and what will give you hope, is that instruments can be specialized. What do I mean? The guitar, more so than other instruments, is specialized. Not everyone can play multiple styles, and that's fine. Once again, if everyone played the same things or played in the same ways, music would be super boring.

The same principles apply to how we learn. Everyone has a different learning style, including you. Each person also possesses their own specific areas of talent. That is why at Rob's School of Music we specialize in creating custom lesson paths for each student. As an educator, it's my job to get information to each person in a way that they can understand.

Don't let your present ability, which was hard earned I'm sure, intimidate you out of progressing on your own journey. Think about what it would be like to be able to watch John Mayer learn to play the guitar. Do you think he was amazing right away? No, he had to practice and unfold his talents and develop his style just like any other musician. Does he have more natural talent playing the guitar? Sure. But the great thing about music is that with practice, anyone can learn to create it, even if they don't have a ton of natural talent.

Sometimes I sit and think about what it would be like if we did have a social-media vault full of videos where John was learning to play the guitar. Wouldn't that be awesome? When I was young we didn't have access to the same technology that's available now. So I don't have a ton of evidence of how I've progressed as a musician over the years. But you can keep track of it all!

Your journey is your story, and stories are what cause powerful points of connection to happen. Stories are dynamic. With a story, you can do just about anything. And right now, you are building your musical story, one note at a time. Don't let anyone diminish that journey for you, including that intimidating voice in your head that says you can't.

Allow yourself the space and time to build your own story. We all have a starting point—a genesis. This is your time to allow yourself to learn, to make mistakes, and to become the version of yourself—and nobody else's—that you want to be.

MANAGING EXPECTATIONS AND DETERMINING YOUR PROGRESS

A lot of the time, we aren't good at measuring the progress we've made. It's also difficult to manage expectations when you're first starting out. This is why having a teacher/mentor is super helpful. You have someone who knows what you're trying to learn and can help you set realistic goals. Plus, you have someone in your corner who will help you exit your comfort zone when you've gotten better and can level up your playing.

One time I was teaching a guitar student and she started humming as she was strumming on her guitar. I asked her, "What is that?" Well, she sang me something, and as it turned out, she had a fantastic voice that I had never heard before that moment. I asked her why I had never heard her sing. Her answer saddened me more than I can say, because it's something I've heard all too often.

She told me that she didn't sing because she had been told her entire life that she wasn't a good singer by people whose opinions really mattered to her: important men and women in her life. So, she was nervous to sing because so many people had used their words to stomp down her magnificent voice. I couldn't let her keep hiding her amazing talent, so I asked her to write a song about what she had been through.

When she finished and shared the song with me, I cried and cried. In that moment she overcame the past with such power and force because she found the courage to move forward through her voice: the one thing that so many people she loved had tried to silence. Now, she's not just a guitar student, she's a voice student, too.

Just because someone tells you something doesn't mean that what they are saying is true. If you get feedback and you aren't satisfied with where you are, you can always do the work to level up. You can always learn to be like my student and use the thing people said wasn't good enough to prove them wrong. Find your power. Find your voice. Once you do that, you can do anything.

Summary

- One of the only things you can control is whether or not you quit.
- It is vital to choose inspiration instead of intimidation when you encounter a musician who is better than you are.
- Social media musicians sometimes use tricks to make them appear to play faster or better. The only safe person for you to compare yourself to is you in the past.
- Instead of thinking I'll never be that good, you can choose to think They've found their thing, and that's awesome, and I can also find mine.
- Everyone has a different learning style.
- It's good to have a mentor to challenge you.
- Sometimes the important voices in your life are wrong. It never hurts to get an outside opinion. It's especially important to get the opinion of a trusted mentor.

Discussion Questions

1. What things can you control in life? What things are outside your control?
2. How can you choose to respond in a way that leaves you inspired instead of intimidated?
3. Who should you compare yourself to? How can you measure progress?
4. If someone says something, does that mean what they say is automatically true? Who can you trust to tell you the truth?

Rob's Music Notes –
Intro to Music Theory

The wonderful thing about music is that it's a paradox: The two following things I'm going to say sound like they contradict each other but they don't. Music is distinct, however it's also universal. That's how magical music really is. In one way, music creates a sharp focus on cultural expression. Have you ever noticed that music in different regions of South America sounds different? The rhythms and patterns you hear in Argentinian music are different from what you would hear in Peruvian music. It's that way in every corner of the world, no matter which continent you're on. In another way, music creates a universal language based solely on math. You don't need to understand what the other person is saying to figure out what time signature they're using or what note they're playing in. It's a way of communicating that transcends culture altogether.

WHAT IS MUSIC THEORY?

Music is a system of creating sounds based on notes, scales, and beats. And because there are so many people who want to understand how to approach music, people have created something called "Music theory," which helps us understand how to interpret the ways notes, beats, melodies, and harmonies work together to create music. Music theory is a tool that gives us the language we need in order to communicate musical ideas. If you learn it and use it often enough, you will be able to understand and speak about it without using so much brain power.

We're going to start with the absolute most basic idea you need to know about music theory. When you hear a sound, what's really happening is that a vibration has traveled through the air and been received by your ear. Your brain can then interpret that as a sound, and you "hear" it. Musically speaking, we categorize sounds by referring to them as "notes" based on where they fall according to how fast the vibration occurs. If it the vibration is fast, the note is high. If the vibration is slow, the note is low.

12 Notes

In most of the songs you've heard, there are 12 notes that the musicians use. For ease, we've given each of these 12 notes names by using letters. If you're looking at a keyboard and you're wondering why there are way more than 12 keys, that's because we can use these same notes moving faster or slower. The crazy thing is that your brain recognizes automatically that these vibration speeds are related. So, for example, if you hear a middle C and then a C 12 notes away, your brain knows they're the same note. They're just expressed at different speeds of vibration. The brain is pretty cool, right?

The space between one note and the same note twice as fast is 12 away, which is called an octave. The space between any note is called a half step. The space between two half steps is called a whole step.

In the next chapter I'm going to break down how to use this knowledge to adjust things if you play a note that sounds wonky by teaching you about keys and scales, but for now, I want you to focus on the overall picture. Keys on the piano represent individual notes. But when you talk about what key you're playing in, you're talking about the letter of the note you want to play and its friends that are compatible with that note. These friends come together to make the scale.

Chords are made out of notes that are grouped together in different ways according to the scale of the key you're playing in. When we play the guitar, we create chords by pressing certain strings on specific frets along the fretboard and leaving other strings open, or untouched. We can also mute strings by pressing on them lightly so that they don't make any sound when played. When we play chords on the piano, we use the piano keys that fit within the scale based on different mathematical patterns.

TEMPO

Mathematical models leave behind why certain chords sound sad while other ones sound happy. While math plays a role in the way the notes are related to each other and played together in a chord, math is also involved in tempo (the speed of the notes you're playing). This is the when of the note that is played. If you've ever heard a drummer click their sticks four times while counting, "One, two, three, four," you understand that in order for everyone to play together, they need to have a joint starting point. That's what the drummer is helping them do, start together. The drummer also helps the musicians stay together as they play through the song.

In any song, the speed, or tempo, can change as the song progresses. The members in the band will listen to the drummer for those cues. When an orchestra plays, they watch the conductor's hand movements to help them understand when to slow down (called a ritardando) or speed up (called an accelerando).

Tempo on written music is displayed by using numbers. Common time, also known as 4/4, means that each measure of time is made up of four beats. Most popular songs you hear use common time. Next time you hear a song on the radio, try counting "one, two, three, four" during the song. Every time you start over, that's a new measure or bar on a piece of sheet music. There are other kinds of timing, like 3/4, 5/4, or 6/8, but for the purposes of this book, you don't really need to worry about them.

You Can Still Shred

If you don't know anything about music theory and this all sounds like gobbledygook to you, don't worry. You can still shred. As you learn about music theory, keys, chords, scales, and tempo, you'll be able to apply the terms you're learning to actual music, and that helps a lot. I just wanted to give you the basics so that you can understand me, or any other music teacher out there, the next time you sit down to jam.

CHAPTER 4

Shut Up & Play - There's No Wrong Way

"Not using a pick came from my dad being really good at playing a Drop D thumb-based drone over the top over what he was playing. I was asking [him] 'How do you finger pick?' because he was really good at it. He said I needed to drop the pick and just do it. So it forced me to come up with my own weird style because he didn't actually show me anything. He just said 'Stop playing with a pick.' The technique is not 'correct', but this became comfortable for me. When you find a way of playing that is natural to you and easy for you, I think your own voice kind of comes through better."

—Arianna Powell *(Arianna has played guitar on stage, in studio, and on live TV with artists like Halsey, Dua Lipa, Olivia Rodrigo, will.i.am, and Lauren Jauregui.)*

One of the things I hear over and over again in the music world is people saying, "You're doing it the wrong way," as if there is some universal absolute about the right way to play music. Honestly, I'm sick of it. The truth is that no matter how you play, as long as you make the sounds you want to come out of the instrument actually come out of it, you're playing right. There is no wrong way to rock and I can prove it.

The single most important thing you for to remember, in music and in life, is that you can always find the opportunity in the situation: even when things seem bleak. To illustrate just how embarrassing or hopeless I'm talking here, let me tell you a story about a time when I was trying to look like David Lee Roth. I think you'll be able to relate. This was one of those moments in my career when a lot of people probably thought I was "doing it wrong."

It all started over a decade ago when tight jeans seemed tighter than ever, and jumping off a drum riser was a mandatory part of looking cool at a rock and roll show. I was playing at the Stone Pony, which is a really cool venue where legends of music history like Bruce Springsteen and Sam Cooke have played.

During the show I decided it was time: I was going to execute a perfect David Lee Roth air-split as I dove from the drum riser. I took a breath, jumped, and nailed it. The crowd went wild! As I continued to shred through the show, though, I realized that somehow the room was getting colder, especially when I thought about myself from the waist down.

As the night went on, the breeze grew, and finally I realized that my pants were split. That air-split had done its job faithfully and ripped the crotch of my pants in a fantastic manner. Thankfully, I was wearing underwear that night. Yes, they were lime green, but they covered what they needed to cover.

Later on, when I watched a video that someone had recorded of the show, I realized that this happened during the second song of our 50-minute set. The hole in my pants grew bigger each minute. I had played a super crowded show at the historically famous Stone Pony with a very large and growing hole in my crotch for almost an hour.

I could have decided that the embarrassment of that moment, which was caught on video, was too much. That after years of pouring myself into music, the fact that my neon green undies having been seen by almost a thousand people meant it was time to give up. But you know what? Life happens.

Now I laugh about and use it as a fun story to tell my students (and you apparently). In that moment, I was presented with the opportunity to get over myself. I could choose to focus on the fact that I ripped my pants in front of a ton of people, or I could focus on the fact that I nailed the air-split and played an awesome show in a packed-out venue.

Jumping off the drum riser wasn't wrong. It was risky, sure. But it was an opportunity I had to take, and I'm glad I did. Ripping my pants wasn't a choice I made, but I was able to choose what to do after the fact. Sometimes, though, you get to choose ahead of time.

Natural and Easy Is Relative

When I interviewed Arianna Powell for the Rob's School of Music YouTube channel, I knew that I had to ask her about her unique way of playing the guitar without a pick. Right now, I have a student who doesn't like playing with a pick, so I showed her a few musicians like Yvette Young and Arianna because they don't use picks in a traditional sense. Now this student can create her own hybrid way to play based on what's comfortable to her. A lot of people would say she's doing it wrong, but she's doing what works for her, and that's never wrong in music.

In the world in general and in music education, there are traditional techniques that everyone teaches. One example would be that you must hold your guitar pick between your finger and thumb, parallel to the strings. But when you think of how Eddie Van Halen plays, you realize he doesn't do that. He holds his pick between his thumb and a combination of his index and middle fingers with his wrist high above the bridge and strings. Do you think that anyone would have the guts to tell Eddie he's playing wrong? No, because he's playing the way that works for him and obviously it serves him well.

There are guitar teachers out there who will tell you that your thumb has to be dead center on the back of the guitar all the time. That's not true. I have learned how to adapt my teaching based on decades of real-world experience playing thousands of gigs as a professional around the USA. When you're playing a show and running and jumping around, you can't keep your thumb dead center on the back of the neck. In fact, some people use their thumbs to play, too.

The question I keep asking is, "Why isn't everyone teaching that way?" And since no one learns the same, teachers need to be ready to adapt and evolve their techniques according to the student's style. Unfortunately, that just doesn't happen often enough.

I believe that music is full of hundreds—if not thousands—of really strong suggestions, but very few absolutes. There's beauty in doing it your own way, which is what Arianna describes in the quote at the beginning of this chapter. In fact, if people didn't look for more tailored ways to play that made them feel more natural, there would never be any new techniques.

Think about what would have happened if Tom Morello had taken his guitar cable out of his guitar to move it around on his bridge using his wah pedal to play a solo for the first time on stage, and some dude stood up and yelled that he was doing it wrong. Well, I imagine that wouldn't have gone very well for whoever did that because the fans would have probably escorted him out after Tom rightly offering the dude some justified choice language. But thinking of things as right and wrong kills any chance music has of being a creative outlet.

People don't play music to be bored by doing everything just right. People play music to have fun. Anytime Tom Morello plays his guitar that way, it's awesome! It's right because of how wrong it is. This is proof that there is no wrong way.

I'm left-handed, but I play the guitar like a righty. It's actually a guitar superpower because both of my hands work so well at the same time. There's no guaranteed formula for how to play anything. You can strum up and down four times in a bar, eight times, sixteen times. These options all bring different things to your musicality. That doesn't mean any of them is wrong or right.

It's vital for you to keep moving forward. Don't get trapped into thinking about the way things should be. Think about how they are for you right now, and keep going.

Everything is Building Toward Something

Many students have what I like to call "analysis paralysis." If you try to make something perfect, you will never end up with anything complete. There are a million unfinished songs written in notebooks and on scraps of paper all over the world. What people don't think about when they leave so many projects unfinished is that the more you create, the better you get at it.

Whether you're learning to play a rock ballad or writing your own first song, perfection isn't realistic. But your second song will definitely be better than your first because you're learning. Your third song will be even better, and so will your fifth. Don't stop working on new things. You can always go back and rework old projects, but learning music is an accumulative process.

When Limp Bizkit had just started playing "Nookie," my band was playing one of those pay-to-play shows where you sell a certain number of tickets to guarantee your stage time. We were one of the first bands on, and we decided to close with "Nookie." (Hey, don't judge me. You never know which of the songs you love right now will seem embarrassing later.) The truth is, we messed it up in a catastrophic fashion. It's not something we had rehearsed a lot because it was brand new. In that moment, I realized that we could go out with a bomb, or we could try to salvage our set. I turned around to my bandmates and said "Just keep going. I'll make it work." I sang the chorus into the microphone again and then held it out to the crowd so they could sing the second half. After this happened a few times, the crowd went crazy. Then the band all came back in together and the place exploded!

Could we play the song perfectly? Obviously not. But we made it our own, we tried something new, and in the end, it was magical. The call and response thing worked. I sang and the crowd sang back. There was this huge mosh pit surging all around us, and we were all connected in that moment through a popular song we could all appreciate together. It was a relevant moment and the crowd was excited that we brought it to them. We transferred our energy to them and they gave it back.

Those moments are enough to help you remember why you do what you do as a musician. If you use these little moments like power-ups to keep you going when you're down, you'll get a recharge that can last until you get a new moment. Music is a lifestyle, not a hobby, and there are magic moments like the one I just described out there in the world just waiting for you.

Summary

- Too many people criticize new music students by saying "You're doing it the wrong way," but there's no universal truth about the right way versus the wrong way.
- You can always find an opportunity in any situation, no matter how bleak.
- It's more important to be true to yourself than to seem perfect. Even if that means showing a packed venue your lime green underwear.
- Life happens, but you get to choose how you respond.
- When you choose to embrace what is natural and easy to you, other people might say you're doing it wrong. Ignore them!

- Music is full of hundreds if not thousands of really strong suggestions, but very few absolutes.
- Tom Morello is an absolute role model.
- Everything is building toward something. Don't get stuck trying to achieve perfection. Keep going and you'll get better.
- Loving and playing music will occasionally reward you with magic moments that keep you going. Pocket those and use them like power-ups when you have a hard day.

DISCUSSION QUESTIONS

1. Is there really a wrong way to play music?
2. When you make a mistake or something embarrassing happens, is it worth quitting over?
3. Is the same way of playing natural and easy to everyone, or are there different playing styles?
4. Should your goal be perfection? If not, what should your goal be?
5. What is "analysis paralysis" and how can it stop you from shredding?

ROB's MUSIC NOTES –
A HALF STEP AWAY & THE GUITAR LEARNING ARC

In this music note, we're going to get a little technical, but don't panic. I'm going to walk you through the 12 notes in the musical alphabet because I need you to understand something super important: even if you're "wrong" you're just a half step away from success. Let's do this!

The 12 notes we use repeatedly in music can be represented by a collection of letters we call the musical alphabet along with sharps and flats. I'll explain more about sharps and flats in a minute, but before we get to that, I want to introduce you to the main characters in your musical journey: the notes.

THE 12 NOTES IN THE MUSICAL ALPHABET

A, A#, B, C, C#, D, D#, E, F, F#, G, G#

That's it. Now, let's take a tiny detour to talk about sharps and flats like I promised. In the list above, you can see the "#" mark. And before that was popular for marking social media posts, its main purpose was to identify sharps in music. We musicians still use it that way. Flats are symbolized using a tiny slanted lowercase "b" and that symbol looks like this: ♭. Sharps and flats communicate something to us about which direction the note that has that symbol attached to it moves a half step away from that letter. So, for example, when I talk about C sharp, that means you are playing the note that has gone up half a step past the C note. If I say A flat, that means the note has gone down half a step past the A note. Sharps and flats are called "Enharmonic Notes."

The best way to remember which notes in the 12-note lineup have sharps is to use a mnemonic device, which is just a fancy way of saying you made up a funny or clever sentence to help you remember each letter. I teach my students to memorize this phrase: big elephants don't do sharps. This means that there are no sharps for B or E: Big Elephants.

These 12 notes are the same ones that everyone in contemporary music has used over the past hundreds of years: The Beatles, Billie Eilish, Beethoven, etc. They all had the same notes, and now you do, too.

Every song has a key and that key produces a scale of notes, just like we talked about in the music note from Chapter 3. Now we can get a little further into how keys and scales work. Every song has a key (remember, not the key on a piano, this key has to do with the lettered note you're using). Each key produces a scale of notes. There are 7 notes in any major or minor scale.

For example, the key of C major contains the notes C, D, E, F, G, A, B, and C again. The last C is 8 steps higher than the first C, and this represents an octave. In the last note we talked about how your brain can understand different notes as vibrating twice as fast or twice as slow. The first C in the scale of C major is vibrating half as fast as the second C in the scale.

Since music is a mathematical language, then it makes sense that music also uses formulas. The formula for a major scale is determined by the spaces between the notes. This is a great first pattern to memorize and looks like this:

Whole note, Whole note, Half note, Whole note, Whole note, Whole note, Half note

or W W H W W W H

In the image below, you can see what this would look like on a piece of sheet music, and below that, on a guitar's fret-board.

Intervals of the Major Scale

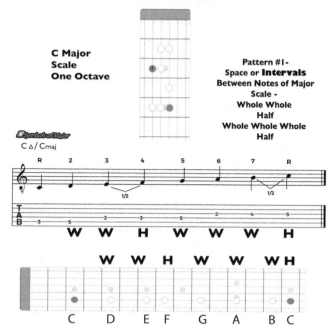

If you count the number of notes in the key of C major, there are 7. And that's a good number to remember because every major and minor scale is made out of 7 notes, and remember: there are only 12 notes in the musical alphabet. This means that if you randomly play any arbitrary note on the neck of a guitar, you have over a 50% chance of that note being in the key you're playing. I don't know about you, but this percentage encourages me. I have more than a one-in-two chance that I'll accidentally pick a note in the scale of the key I'm playing.

On the other hand, let's say I accidentally play a note that is outside of the scale. What then? Do I throw down my guitar and quit music forever? Of course not. All you have to do if you hit one of the notes outside the scale for the key you're in is shift up or down (away from your body or toward your body on the same string) one half step, which is one fret. That's it! Talk about awesome, right? Even if you make a mistake—which odds are you're more likely to get it right—you can adjust quickly and easily. No matter what, you're only a fret away!

WHEN "WRONG" SOUNDS RIGHT

Have you ever heard a song by the Electric Light Orchestra? What about twenty one pilots? Both of these bands utilize "wrong" notes to create interesting sounds that trigger the curiosity of their listeners.

These interesting notes that don't fit into the scale of the key they are playing can be perceived as intriguing. This tension keeps the audience listening until you get to the catchier, more mainstream-sounding choruses.

When Bob Dylan first started playing the electric guitar, people thought, "Oh, that's wrong." But the only reason they perceived it as wrong was because they were used to him playing the acoustic guitar. But it wasn't wrong, it was just different. Now we hear Bob Dylan playing the electric guitar and we love it!

Keep in mind that wherever you end up on the fret-board, you need to ask yourself "How can I make this work? Where is the opportunity to be found here?" There is no "wrong" in music. You just have to be willing to find creative solutions. Always be looking for the opportunity you can find in what other people label as wrong.

THE GUITAR-LEARNING ARC

Because this note is all about learning to work through the obstacles that come up when you first start playing, I think it's the perfect place to talk about the guitar-learning arc. I'm just using the guitar as an example. Other instruments have their own learning arcs. What I love about the guitar, though, is that the arc is relatively short. I have no idea how long the arc would be on something like a French horn, but if you play one, write me an email and let me know.

Whenever you start a new journey in life, you have to tell yourself from the beginning that you will work through the crappy part. There is always a crappy part, guaranteed. When you first learn how to bake, your recipes don't always turn out great. Sometimes you add too much baking soda and your cookies end up tasting like chocolate-chip cupcakes. I'm not saying that happened to me, but I'm not denying it either.

The same principle is true when the time comes to pick up your first guitar. It's a three-month long process starting from zero. In those first 12 weeks, you are going to feel uncomfortable. You won't feel like a rock star, yet. Your fingers will hurt like hell. That's why it is vital for you to decide you won't quit even before you start. You have to keep going.

When month two hits, your fingers will still hurt like hell. Your brain will be fighting you as you make your way through the frets and struggle to press the right strings. Nothing will feel like it's clicking.

Finally, sometime in month three, your brain starts to catch up to your hands. Things shift into place so much that by your fourth or fifth month, you won't even remember how crazy hard it was when you started. And your fingers will have developed calluses that will make it so you can play without the hurting-like-hell part.

This magical arc will only work if you practice as much as I tell you to, though. So, how long do you

Playing Doesn't Always Equal Practicing

When you're first starting out, it's time to create good habits right away. You need to have at least four 30-minute practices a week. On top of this, I advise one guitar lesson per week. If you do this, you'll be practicing for two hours a week. But you can't just do anything in practice. You need to spend one-third of every 30-minute session—just 10 minutes—working on something that challenges you. Something that's hard and probably even makes you feel frustrated.

Most musicians pick up their guitar and play their favorite thing, which is good because anytime your instrument is in your hand, you're slowly getting better. But if you use 10 minutes of that time to play something difficult, after 12 months, you'll be better than most players who have been playing for at least three years.

Something that bums me out is when I see people who say they've been playing for 20, 30, or even 40 years play the same way they probably did when they first started out. Using years as a metric is vague, because time doesn't necessarily equal skill. What really matters is how you've been playing. You don't want to stay playing at the same level year after year, do you? The trick is you have to be willing to push yourself.

Is using this method difficult? Yes, but only if you try to do it alone. I provide accountability and support to my students so that they can make it through this process successfully. I'm not saying that if you want to play the guitar well that you have to wait 12 to 18 months. You will be able to shred way sooner than that. But if you want to unlock the next level in your guitar-learning journey, you need to be willing to push through those moments when you feel frustrated and want to quit. You need to put in the work, and play things that will make you better in addition to just playing things that you already know.

R. Spampinato

CHAPTER 5

Everything or Nothing? How to Follow Your Dreams While Living with Purpose

"There's never a shortage [of] things to learn."
–Richard Fortus (*Richard has been playing guitar with Guns N' Roses since 2002*)

Have you ever heard people talk about dedicating their lives to one thing? A lot of students come into my school wanting to focus all their thoughts and energy on becoming a badass musician. I get it, because I've been there too. But the more I look back at my own story, the more I think about how I wouldn't have gotten to where I am now if there hadn't been more than just music in my life. In fact, I would have never gotten back into music if it wasn't for my karate class. Does that sound weird? I can explain.

HOW KARATE INFLUENCED MY MUSICAL LIFESTYLE

You remember that when I was five, my dad got me my first guitar. You probably also remember that I never got past the finger-hurting stage and my teacher didn't find a way to connect with me. That's when I quit and my dad tossed my little Strat knock-off into our front yard. But my musical journey didn't end there. Why? Because of karate.

When I was nine years old, my parents got me into karate. The truth is, up until then, I was never really confident in who I was. I was pretty tall for my age, but I didn't have much muscle, so I didn't feel like I could stand up for myself. The guy who taught me karate, Mike C., didn't just teach me what my parents paid him to: sure, I learned to kick, block, and punch with the rest of them. Mike taught me so much more.

The job of a teacher is to take people who aren't great at whatever they come to you needing help for, and to coach them to the point where they improve. Since I was so tall, Mike put me into the adult karate class. I wasn't too thrilled about that at the time because I was still really young. I felt out of place in that class at first.

I can say with confidence that nothing in life has ever come easily or naturally to me. The same was true for karate. But instead of telling me I didn't have any natural talent and sending me away, Mike C. told me I could 100% learn how to do karate. Like everything else in my life, it took a lot of hard work to learn, but because I had Mike, I kept going.

Those Sunday mornings at karate with Mike didn't just teach me how to use my body in a productive way through repetition and technique. Those classes were also my first lessons on how to teach. Mike modeled the same teaching methods with me back then that I use with my students today. And I wouldn't have learned that without karate.

But don't forget that karate also gave me James Mirarchi and Brian Winder, who are still my best friends all these years later. If it hadn't been for James and Brian and their passionate obsession with music, it probably would have taken me a lot longer to pick my guitar back up.

If James had been singularly focused on music though, I never would have met him in my karate class. In fact, when I first met him and he told me he wanted to be in a band, I remember thinking, Why would anyone ever want to be in a band? They're never going to be able to achieve any fame or greatness or whatever. But now music is my career in addition to being my passion. You never know what things outside of music are going to give you some of the biggest gifts in your life. Karate gave me both James and my learned love for teaching.

The Job of a Good Teacher

The job of a good teacher isn't just to take people who want to get better at something and help them do that. That isn't all that Mike C. did for me in those Sunday morning karate lessons. And now that I'm a teacher, too, I try to remember that whenever I work with my students.

My first goal as a teacher is always to make my students feel comfortable. Sometimes that's more difficult depending on each person. It's my job to break down any barriers that exist between me and my students. One of the ways I do this is to remember, and emphasize, that we are all constant students, including me. Any time I sit down at the guitar or the drums, I'm there to learn something. I need my students to know that I make mistakes so that they will understand that mistakes are part of how we all learn.

The primary thing I'm trying to convey to my students is that they have every reason to be confident. If they feel like they can do what I'm teaching them to do, they're more likely to practice. If they believe in themselves, they'll be able to make progress.

Any time any one of my students does something awesome, which always happens at least once during each lesson, I react. That's part of my personality. I get loud when I'm excited. It is also a part of my personal nature to rejoice with others when something amazing happens for them.

When I get new students, sometimes their parents will see my reaction and accuse me of being so outgoing because I want to keep their kid as a student. This makes me sad because it always causes me to wonder if they aren't rejoicing with their kid when super cool things happen. That's what kids need because that's what we all need: cheerleaders. No, not necessarily the kind with pom-poms.

On the flip side, though, a good teacher will also tell you when there's something you need to fix. I definitely don't skip that step. I also provide real accountability for my students, just like Mike provided that for me when I was younger. When someone cares about you, they're going to tell you the truth. So when you're doing well, they'll say "Hey, you're doing great," but when you need work they'll say "You could spend a little more time practicing that one part."

Since I'm trying to live up to Mike's impact in my life, I also take an extra step to help my students find balance. Whenever I meet a new student, I always ask them "What is your thing outside of music?" Sometimes they look at me for a minute and ask what I mean. "Well, you know, like drawing or basketball or something. My thing outside of music is being outside. I have to be out in the open air every morning. It's really important to me that I spend time out in nature."

I want my students to know that if they focus solely on music, they are going to get burned out.

They are also going to miss out on cool relationships and hobbies that are likely to make them even better musicians. And that leads us to the final question in this chapter.

CAN YOU DO BOTH?

Can you do both of what? The question here, that a lot of students ask, is related to wanting to make it in music as a professional who plays gigs or does studio work and having things in your life that aren't music-related.

The simple truth is, whatever your main thing in life turns out to be, you need other things too. I was talking with my writer friend about this the other day. She's a professional writer and writing coach, and she also loves music. When I was talking to her about this chapter, she told me that when writers get together, they also ask each other the same question I ask my students: "What is your thing outside of writing?" She said that a lot of times, the answer for writers is, "I play music." Isn't that interesting?

I have a theory that creative people especially need to be involved in more than just one kind of expressive thing. At my music school, I meet a ton of creative people, because if you aren't creative, you usually aren't drawn to music. But don't be fooled into thinking that art teachers are the only creative types out there. People who like to express themselves through art, music, and writing come in all different packages. Just because someone loves to spend all day creating digital worlds on their computer screen doesn't mean they can't jam with the best of them.

I want you to start thinking outside the box when you think about what kinds of people play music, mainly because I don't want you to put yourself inside of a box. There is no way you should dress or talk that either does or doesn't qualify you to learn how to make music. Don't let anyone tell you differently. And definitely don't let your own voice tell you that you don't fit the musical-type cliché that lives in someone else's head. There isn't any one way musicians look or act.

It's weird for me to think about music being the other thing, because music is my main thing. But this just goes to prove that no matter what your main thing is, you need to have something outside of it to balance you out. Getting super focused on only one thing can actually cause you to get obsessed with becoming super successful or famous at that one thing, and that just sucks the fun and thrill right out of doing what you love.

So now, I want to ask you: What is your thing outside of music? If you can't think of anything, it's time to branch out and add a new hobby to your activity list. Be creative. Have fun. Get out of your comfort zone so you can grow not just as a musician, but as a person.

Summary

- You don't know when or where you're going to learn the most important lessons of your life so be open.
- If you don't naturally have talent at something, you can always work hard and learn how to do it.
- If you want to accelerate your learning process, it's important to have a teacher who will help you improve.
- You never know when or where you're going to find your best friend or the person that helps you find your true passion in life.
- It is not healthy to be focused on only one thing. Life is too short and there are too many awesome things to try.
- Without confidence, it's difficult to make progress in whatever you're doing.
- People need others to rejoice with them when they get something right. They also need honest people around to help them adjust when they need to keep working to get there.
- You can have more than just your one main thing. In fact, it's important to have something else because then it's harder to get obsessed with succeeding at that one thing.
- Everyone needs balance.

DISCUSSION QUESTIONS

1. Think back on the journey of your own life. What things outside of music have inspired you?

2. Have you found your James (best friend)? Think about where you found them and write it down.

3. Do you want to get better faster? Have you ever thought about hiring a teacher to help you do that? Why or why not?

4. What is your thing outside of music? How does it help you live a more balanced life?

Rob's Music Notes –
SETTING SMART GOALS

In these notes, I love sharing practical stuff with you. But this note in particular will move you forward not only in your musical aspirations: I'm going to show you how to accomplish anything you want in life, all with five SMART letters.

SMART GOALS

The reason we want to set SMART goals instead of just goals in general is because using each word that makes up the acronym "SMART" gives us a way better chance of actually getting what we want out of life. Let's learn what SMART is, one letter at a time.

A lot of people will say things to me like, "I want to be like Dave Grohl someday." I totally get it.

Dave Grohl is awesome. It's hard for me to imagine something Dave can't do. But that's not really a goal that you can go after. In order to set goals you can actually achieve, you need to be specific before you do anything else. And that's why "S" is the first letter in SMART. Your goal has to be specific.

SPECIFIC

When you say something like "I want to be the next Dave Grohl," it's too vague. Honestly, Dave is just too many cool things. He's one of the best drummers in the world. He's a veteran guitarist. He's got pipes for days. In addition to all those things and being a prolific songwriter, he's also a super cool dad. Some of his kids even tour with him.

So, what do you mean when you say you want to be like Dave? Let's assume you mean his drumming prowess. So you want to be a drummer, huh? You're about to be part of a very diverse and awesome club. Welcome. I caught the drumming bug from my dad, who still kills it with sticks by the way.

Even saying "I want to be a drummer" is too general, though. You need to think about what kind of drummer you want to be. You want something like, "I want to learn to be a jazz drummer who specializes in studio sessions." Or, "I want to be a drummer who goes on a tour a couple of times a year with an awesome metal band." Or even, "I want to play percussion in a famous symphony. Someone has to make those cymbals clang!"

In order to get your answer as specific as you need it to be, think about these questions.

Who? What? When? Where? Which? Why?

Who is involved? Who do you need around in order to make what you want to happen become reality? When I was thinking about my karate goals, I needed a teacher. That person ended up being Mike C.

What? Think through what you want to do. Get as detailed as possible! Honestly, the more you can fine-tune this answer, the better.

When? You will get super specific about this question when you get to the "T" in SMART, but for now, set a general time frame. Saying, "I want to be an awesome jazz drummer someday" isn't going to help you gain the forward momentum you need.

Where? Sometimes you need to be in a physical location to get closer to your goals. Remember Arianna? She decided to move to where the gigs were and that made a huge difference for her as far as reaching her goals.

Which? Think about the things you need in order to get to this goal. For example, if you wanted to be a dentist (because teeth are just as vital as rock 'n' roll), you would need to go to school first. You can't just roll up to a dentist's office and be like, "Hey, I'd like to be able to pull people's teeth out." What are the requirements for your goal? If you want to be a gig player, you need to have experience. That means you need to go out, find people to gig with, practice, and play shows.

Why? This is probably the most important question you can ask yourself because when things get hard, the answer to the question is what will keep you going. Why is this goal important to you? Is there a specific group of people you want to help? Does this goal give you magic moments that you can use as power-ups when you're having a hard day? What is your why? Remember, the more specific you can be, the better.

Measurable

The "M" in SMART stands for measurable. If you can't measure whether you've gotten closer to your goal, how can you complete it? The reason why you need to come up with numbers to help you understand when you've met your goal is because otherwise you will be running toward a finish line that doesn't exist. For example, during the pandemic I started a YouTube channel for my students. One of my goals was to get more subscribers. If I hadn't set a physical number, like 10,000, how would I ever know when "more" was enough?

If you can't measure your goals, you are way more likely to feel like you aren't getting anything done. And when you feel that way, it's really easy to stop trying.

When it comes to your musical goals, think about how many practice sessions you want to complete, how many lessons you want to work through, and how many months you want to keep up with your practice routine. As you saw in the last note, if you want to be more seasoned than the average guitar player, you need to keep up a 2-hours-a-week practice routine for around 18 months. Write down your end date somewhere and then celebrate when you successfully hit that marker.

ACHIEVABLE

Have you ever sat down and looked at whether your goal was something you could achieve using the tools I've already mentioned? For example, writing "Be a Grammy winning musician," isn't something you can set specific goals to work for because there are complicated processes behind the scenes that are outside of your control.

"Achievable" isn't supposed to bum you out, though a lot of people get hung up on this one. They'll say "Well, it seems like none of my goals are achievable, then." But that's not true. Remember your practice goals? You want to be doing one lesson and then practicing 2 hours every week. That is definitely an achievable goal because you can literally measure whether you're putting in the time. There isn't anyone behind the scenes like there would be if you were trying to win a Grammy. A whole board of people decide that, so it's not something you can measure.

You also can't expect to be able to go on tour with Journey or Guns N' Roses if you don't have the skills to play at that level yet. So whatever goal you set, think of both long-term and short-term things. If the goal you want long-term isn't something you can do yet because you lack the skills, make your short-term goals center around learning those skills. Think about what steps you would need to take to level up your skill set. Then revisit your big goals to see if they're attainable once you've gotten the achievable part worked out.

RELEVANT

In the last section, we talked about how if you don't have the skills you need to accomplish your long-term goals, you need to get them. When you think about "R" and what's relevant, you need to focus on the long-term goal you have in order to make sure that whatever short-term items appear on your list will help you get closer to your big-ticket items.

Back when I started giving music lessons, this other teacher had hired me to help and then suddenly said he wanted to retire. He let me buy his old business and I began teaching out of Alto Music—the same shop where my dad had bought all of my instruments growing up. Well, not long after I bought that music teacher's business, my friend who owned the music shop told me he was going to sell it. Then he asked if I wanted to buy it.

I was shocked! And not just by the 1-million-dollar price tag on the store. No matter what, I was going to have to choose something. If I bought the store, I could run it and keep operating my music lessons there. But I hadn't paid off the loan I took out to buy the other music teacher's business from him yet, so the idea of buying the entire store freaked me out. Plus, I wanted to be in the music-teaching business: not the instrument-selling business.

If I didn't buy the music store, I needed another place to teach music lessons because I didn't know if the new owner—whomever bought the place—would let me keep teaching there. I had to look at the next step I needed to take if I wanted to achieve my overall goal of having a music school. So, later that day—once the shock of everything wore off—I called my friend who is a real estate agent and asked her to help me find a place I could turn into a school.

Within a few days we had found the perfect spot and I had convinced the owner to give me a lease (my rocker persona doesn't always give people the impression I'm a super serious entrepreneur even though I am). Rob's School of Music was born. But it wouldn't have been possible if I hadn't found a location to have the school in.

Getting a physical location built out and ready was a smaller goal that was super relevant to me achieving my long-term goal of having a music school.

When you're trying to figure out what your smaller goals are, you need to ask yourself "Is this goal relevant to my bigger goal?" If the answer is "no," then you need to adjust those mini goals until the answer is "yes."

TIME-BOUND

The "T" in SMART is usually referred to as meaning "time-bound" because there isn't really a better way to explain what kind of time-related goal you have with the letter "T". It's still a SMART acronym though (see what I did there?). Any person can write out a list of goals, but if there isn't any timeline involved, there isn't a huge possibility that they will succeed.

You need to look at a calendar and be able to say, "On that date I will have finished this mini goal," or "By March of 20___, I will be able to shred on the guitar by playing [insert specific technically difficult song here]." Every year I set both personal and professional goals for myself and for my business. You'd better believe that these goals have dates attached. The only way to move forward is to know that you're working toward something in real time. Imaginary somedays don't help you set SMART goals.

WHAT ARE YOUR SMART GOALS?

Now that you know how SMART goals work, I want you to write a list of five short-term goals, and two long-term goals. Remember to ask yourself these questions for each goal:

Is it specific enough?

How am I going to measure if I'm meeting this goal?

Do I have the skills to attain it? (This question is for short-term goals. For long-term goals you're working your way there.)

Are my short-term goals relevant to my long-term goals?

Do I have a time set when I need to finish each goal by?

You've got this. I believe in you! And if you're having a rough time believing in yourself right now, use my belief in you and keep going!

CHAPTER 6

Rock Star Shield of Armor – Banishing Doubt One Thought at a Time

"What makes it even harder now in this generation is that everybody's got a camera, right? And everybody can look on YouTube for that past performance that you hope no one ever got to see. But it's just life now and you just accept it. Sometimes you make mistakes, and that's okay. It's just human. Everybody makes mistakes. So you just have to be confident that you're going in as prepared as possible."

–Cory Churko *(Cory is a music director and plays both the fiddle and the guitar. He has done both studio and live work with artists such as Shania Twain, Slash, Kelly Clarkson, and Reba McEntire)*

Whether you want to be a rock star, a school teacher, or a well-loved vegan chef, there is one thing you absolutely need to have: confidence. But what if you feel like confidence in yourself is in short supply? Well, I have a secret trick, and I want to share it with you because it changed everything for me. The first step to being confident is to practice, practice, and practice some more. Know your stuff before you ever step out on stage. I already mentioned this in another chapter, but as you can see in the quote above, Cory Churko agrees with me. So, that part wasn't really a secret. So what is the secret? Keep reading to find out.

Since we're getting to know each other better, there's something I want to confess to you. The truth is, I'm shy. I'm introverted. You wouldn't think so when you see me on stage or watch me interact with my students, but I need alone time every day. Meeting new people makes me anxious. Until I learned how to be confident through my karate lessons with Mike C., I couldn't interact with people the same way I do now. So what changed? There were two big things.

First, having Mike as a mentor meant that I knew there was someone out in the world, other than my parents, who believed in me. Parents are great, but when you have supportive parents, you sort of think it's their job to love you and tell you that you can do amazing things. This means that you don't tend to believe them the same way you would someone else when they say, "Just be yourself! Everything else will fall into place." Mike told me the same things, but it sounded different when he said it. Even when I couldn't manage to believe in myself, I could borrow Mike's belief in me.

Second, I learned how to create a persona to behave the way I would have if I was as confident as that persona was. This is the secret I mentioned earlier. I call this technique "putting on my rock-star persona." This character I created acts like a jacket I can put on and take off when I need it. Rob the rock star is a different person than Rob Spampinato, and that's okay. Rob the rock star is confident. He knows that he worked hard to acquire his shredding and drumming skills. He is not afraid to do an air-split off the drum riser, even if he rips his pants. Rob the rock star can walk into conversations with B-level and A-level musicians and not care if they don't know his name (yes, there's a story coming for this one).

Rob Spampinato is quieter and more thoughtful. Rob the rock star jumps out of his chair when one of his students finally nails the lick they've been working on for three months. The simple truth is that Rob the rock star and Rob Spampinato are the same person. But when Rob S. is feeling too in his head about things, Rob the rock star is able to help Rob S. keep moving forward.

CREATING A PERSONA

The idea of creating a persona when you aren't sure how you should act or what you should do is nothing new. Even the most famous personalities use personas. For example, think about Lady Gaga. Who is she? Well, she's a version of Stefani Joanne Angelina

Germanotta, right? Stefani doesn't disappear from the universe when Lady Gaga performs, does she? No. And music isn't the only space where we see this sort of thing happen.

Think about Tony Robbins. If you don't know who he is, don't worry. I'll tell you right now. He's a super famous speaker, author, and coach who helps people realize their own potential. Go watch a video of him speaking. Once you do, not only will you feel better about yourself, but you'll understand why he has been called in to coach some of the most powerful people in the world. After seeing Tony on stage, do you think that's how intense he is all the time? No. There isn't anyone who could function on that level 24/7 and still have enough energy to exist.

When Tony steps on stage, he puts on his persona as a coach. Russell Brunson, another inspirational entrepreneur who often hangs out with Tony Robbins, explains this phenomenon as "Putting on your attractive character" in his book DotCom Secrets: The Underground Playbook For Growing Your Company Online With Sales Funnels. Brunson has an entire framework dedicated to helping you figure out which attractive character you should be for your business. Since this is a book mostly about rock and roll, I want us to explore the kind of persona that musicians use, including me.

THE FOUNDATION FOR CONFIDENCE

The way I've learned to deal with my shyness—which could have been a potential roadblock for me in my musical career and my job as a music teacher—has been to build out and use a rock-star persona. But how did I do that? Well, in Rob's Music Notes for this chapter, I'm going to walk you step by step through the process so that you can create your own persona. But for now, you need to understand that if you don't have a basis for where your persona's confidence should come from, this technique will not work for you. So, I want to help you build the foundation for that confidence right now.

In order to understand why you should be confident, you need to know that confidence itself is built out of three things inside you that you probably haven't thought about before. All confidence is built around your personhood: what you say (internally and externally), who you know (your support team), and what influence you have in life (your personal power). Since these ideas might be new, let's go through them one at a time.

WHAT YOU SAY

The first piece of confidence you need to know about can be tricky. When I tell you to think about what you say as a person, you might be thinking about the tone of your voice, your grammar, or your accent. But I don't mean any of those things. What I mean is that you need to think about that voice inside that no one else can hear. This little voice tells you all sorts of important things like how you feel and why you feel that way, what is important to you and why, and how you operate uniquely to do you better than anyone else could.

The best part about understanding this voice is that you can start actively deciding who you want to use it with. Maybe you want to put it into a song to share with the world. Or maybe you just want to text your best friend to let them know something new you figured out about yourself. One of the most important things you need to understand about this voice though, is that it can lie.

I want you to answer this question: Does this voice ever keep you from doing the things in life that you really want to do? Remember when I met James and thought about myself "What's the point of being in a band, it's not like I'll ever get a big break or whatever"? That was my voice lying to me. Sometimes what you say is your brain trying to keep you from getting hurt. But that's no way to live.

My voice said to me that I shouldn't join a band. I want to point out that there was insecurity hiding behind that statement. Should I enjoy music even if I don't play on stage with awesome musicians like Rod Castro, Arianna Powell, Richard Fortus, or Rosh

Roslin? Dude, yes! Music is awesome no matter what. Would I love to jam with those people? Of course! But I'm not going to quit music because I don't get to. When I said that thing to myself about how being in a band is pointless if you don't make it big, I was using what we call "limiting beliefs."

Did you know that your brain treats emotional threats like life or death moments? It's true. So when I thought about being in a band, my brain was automatically like, "Okay, Rob. What's the worst-case scenario here? Why shouldn't you risk this?" And it came up with the response that it's only worth playing music in a band if you get famous doing it, and there was little chance of that happening. Now, think about this: What would have happened if I had kept listening to that voice? I would have never known how thrilling, satisfying, and rewarding living a life full of music could be.

A great way to make sure that you aren't letting your little voice lie to you is to run your goals through the SMART filter I taught you in the last chapter. If you can apply SMART to your goal, then you can do it. Don't let your little voice feed you a steady stream of lies.

The things you say in your head and the way you say them matter in general, but those things are even more important when you think about the next part of your confidence: who you know.

WHO YOU KNOW

The truth is, what you say is friends with who you know. If you want to tell the world how you feel, fine, but the world can't really tell you back, can they? The reason that a lot of artists, musicians, and writers get depressed and quit is because they feel like their audiences aren't big enough. They want to know everyone, but that's impossible. The internet did something crazy when it started being used by people on every continent in the world: it destroyed the notion of having a local support group.

We are no longer limited to who we could get to know based on our geographic locations. Maybe you don't understand what it was like before apps and smartphones, but it was different. Not better, not worse, but definitely different. These days, people can look at Instagram and think, "I have 10,000 followers! That means I have 10,000 friends." But that isn't true. What you say only matters when the people who you know also know you back. Healthy relationships are a huge part of being able to build your confidence. Let me ask you a question: How many good friends or relatives do you have in your support group?

I have Brian and James and a bunch of other people. And when I talk to them, I say things I wouldn't say to my YouTube followers. Because they know me back, it makes what I say mean so much more. And when those guys tell me stuff in return, it reminds me that

I'm not alone. Always remember that quantity doesn't equal quality. You need people in your life who know your voice, and whose voices you know. Letting your voice ring out into the world without the context of real relationships won't make you feel heard: it will make you feel empty and lost.

Did you know that you have the power to make your own choices? This ties into both what you say and who you know, so let's take a look at that next.

The Influence You Have in Life

I'm sure you've noticed that there are people out there in the world who don't care what you have to say. They want you to do what they say without question. There are also people who don't care who else you know. These types of people don't want you knowing anyone but them. The word we use for people who behave this way is "manipulative." I'm sure a specific person instantly pops into your head when I use that word. It could be the principal at your school, your boss, or even one of the people who you thought was a good friend.

You need to understand that, from this day forward, no one can impose their influence or power over your decisions. You are in control of your life. You have the influence over yourself to make the decisions you think are best. It can feel really crappy when someone else tries to use their influence to tell you what to do.

In fact, you will probably have people tell you that learning music is a waste of time and that you should do something more serious. What do they mean when they say that anyway? That you should use your spare time and creative resources to study banking? No, you don't have to do that.

There is time to study and there is time to rock out. You don't have to choose one or the other. The point is that the power to choose how you want to live your life is yours and yours alone. If you're a kid, yes, your guardians have a say for now. Hopefully, they are trying to help you figure out how to do life like my parents did with me. But I know that not all guardians are like that. And if yours aren't, I'm sorry. That honestly sucks. But that doesn't mean that you will never be in control of your own life.

Did you know that when you choose how to use your influence, you get to decide whether you want to use that power to tear down or to build up? I choose to build up, and this one thing has made my life so much better. Do I have influence over my students? Yes, because they trust me and establish me as a mentor in their lives. I take that super seriously. And because I have that influence, I make sure to use it for good: just like Mike C. did for me.

It's like I said before, you can choose intimidation or inspiration. Either way, it's your choice. But intimidation is going to weigh you down. Inspiration is going to help you soar to new heights.

MUSIC AND CONFIDENCE

Now you know what confidence is made out of. Awesome. Since you understand that, the next thing I want you to know is that music can actually help you with your confidence. Music can encourage your little voice to stop being so negative. Music can help you find real friends who care about what you feel and think. Music can even give you powerful influence to make the world a better place. How? Let me tell you a story.

Do you remember the guitar student I told you about who had the most important people in her life tell her that she couldn't sing? Yeah, as it turns out, she has the voice of an angel. But she was nervous about me hearing her because of all the negative things she had heard about her singing through the years. It wasn't her own little voice that had lied and told her she wasn't any good at singing, it was the people she knew. And they used their influence with her to try to keep her from singing. That's super messed up, right?

But as you already know, I heard her humming and encouraged her to sing for me. She became a voice student after that. What I didn't tell you about her, though, was how she changed because of that one moment. I think we need to dive a little bit deeper into that interaction for you to understand what I mean.

So, you know that my student was humming a melody to a song we were working on together. I asked her to sing the lyrics instead and she did. They were amazing! She drew me in, and I was curious, so I asked her what the song was about. At that moment, she didn't want to tell me, and that was okay. But I told her, "You know, you drew me in with your words, and that's not easy to do. This is a big win for you." She blushed and a small smile appeared on her face.

You see, I helped her to see herself in a different way. I used my influence in her life to build her up, and she was able to quiet the negative voices she had stored in her head. I helped her see herself in a different way. Just like relationships can destroy, like those people who used their influence with my student to make her think she couldn't sing, relationships can also heal.

At first, she was apprehensive because she was being vulnerable through the creative process of writing a song. She was baring her soul, you know? But I made her understand that she had already done a difficult thing successfully because she wrote those awesome lyrics. But I also needed her to see the truth of how good she is. Without me, she wouldn't have seen that on her own. Music helped us meet each other, and it also helped me prove to her how great she is.

As the lesson progressed, we were able to write a killer bridge because her confidence was through the roof. You see, that's what a good teacher or mentor does, they help you look at yourself through a different lens. A far less critical one. As individuals, we tend to focus on all the things we need to fix about ourselves: our voices, our playing, the way we talk or act. We don't celebrate the small achievements along the way: the brave moments, the challenges we overcome, the new things we learn.

So, I teach my students to celebrate those wins, because when they do, they can more easily recognize their own wins in the future. I want to use my influence for good. I want the people around me to feel like they can accomplish any goal so that they can go out and actually accomplish those goals. If you make people around you feel like failures, they won't be able to meet any goals. The best way to transfer knowledge is through self-confidence. And the best way to feel inspired as a musician is also through self-confidence. Inspiration and self-confidence are best friends.

LOOKS AREN'T IT

One of the things I see my students struggle with—that I've gone through myself—is that people who want to play music feel like they have to fit into the physical description the world has for famous people. Up until recently, this meant thin for girls, ripped for guys, with almost completely symmetrical faces, giant eyes, and "the it factor." Thankfully, that has been changing as we see Hollywood setting the tone for inclusivity and as they put different people of all shapes, sizes, and skin shades in shows, movies, and advertisements.

Unfortunately, a lot of the music world hasn't been as quick to embrace people who don't fit the idea of what people used to say stars should look like.

At Rob's School of Music, we have a singing coach that works especially with teenage girls because she doesn't just want to teach them how to sing. She wants to teach them how beautiful and special they are. Sam (short for Samantha) isn't just another teacher at the school, though. She's also my girlfriend and songwriting partner.

Sam understands what it's like to be a woman in the music industry, because she's been in it for a long time. When she was 14 years old, Disney wanted to sign her, but that wasn't a good fit for her at the time.

Even at that age, she felt the pressure to use her sexuality as a woman to try to find an audience, and she sees how this pressure affects young female musicians every day. But instead of avoiding the music industry because of that, she has leaned into it, but makes sure to do so on her own terms.

During the pandemic, Sam wrote the best part of a song about how it felt to suddenly be in a world of unknowns called "Outbreak." The lyrics use emotional relatability to reach out to people who are all feeling the same way. Because it was a song so many people could relate to, Paul Reed Smith Guitars wrote an article about it online and Grammy Award winning DJ/ Producer Dave Audé created a remix of it that blew up the EDM world.

Instead of relying on objectifying herself by leveraging her sexuality, she uses heartfelt messages and amazing melodies to prove to everyone else that she deserves her space in the music industry. The fact that she has perfect pitch doesn't hurt either.

Over the last eight years, I've watched her transform from a gifted musician to a talented businesswoman as well. The truth is, in this business, there are people who are leeches and jerks. Sam is a bright light. She's a genuinely caring person and I love watching her help her singing students realize their inner rock stars by tapping into the confidence that Sam models every day.

Next time you feel tempted to try to fit yourself into the mold of what music culture says is right and desirable, remember that being you is the best thing you can be. You have things to say. There are people who care about and support you. You can use your own personal influence for good. You are amazing. Don't try to be anyone but you!

YOUR SHIELD OF ARMOR

I always tell my students to use their musical instrument to build a suit of armor. Whether you sing and it's your voice, or you drum and those cymbals are protecting you from those negative thoughts that want to keep you frozen, music can be your active shield.

This armor is just a manifestation of the confidence inside of you. By using this armor, your subconscious lets its guard down. No matter how talented, successful, or athletic someone is, everyone has to sleep. Everyone has to eat and go to the bathroom. Humans are all human. What the persona you build does is give you permission to manifest the person you wish you could be—not just on the inside—but on the outside too. Use your persona like armor so that when you feel afraid, you can banish your doubts. If you do this, you can keep moving forward no matter what else is going on around you or inside your mind.

LEVEL–A VS LEVEL–ME

One of my favorite events on Earth is the National Association of Music Merchants (NAMM) show. You get to see all the newest music technology and a ton of musicians go to this thing to network. It's always a blast. For me, it's been a great way to build relationships and make connections as I grow my business.

Up until 2008, I used to put on physical manifestations of my Rob-the-rock-star persona at this thing, including nail polish and eyeliner. But I didn't care what anyone thought about me, because my persona was engaged. Well, one day at NAMM, I was finally able to test out how far this persona could go.

One of the things that musicians do at NAMM is hang out and eat together. One time, I rock-starred myself into an awkward spot. I was with some friends at the Gibson Guitar party at the Hilton in Anaheim, California. It's right next to the convention center. At NAMM you can see who is an artist, because they give out special black badges with has an "A" for artist on it. I usually get the black badge because I'm endorsed by PRS guitars.

In the music world, one of the ways we identify how serious someone is in the music industry is to give them a letter-rating based on the kind of work they've done. At the Gibson party, I suddenly found myself in a conversation with a couple of B-level musicians, which was fine for me. I didn't feel the least bit intimidated. But then a super-famous A-level musician from the '80s came over to talk to them. Well, I wasn't just going to leave, you know?

So I was sitting there, talking and laughing as A-level told his story. After a while, he started to stare at me. The tiny voice in my head said, "Dude, he's an A-level. You're a you-level. You don't belong here. Time to bolt." It was super clear that the A-level musician had no idea who I was, even though the other guys did.

He told a joke and I laughed. In response, he kind of cocked his head to the side to look at me. Then he noticed my black badge with an "A" on it. He waited with this question on his face, "Who are you?" and I said, "I'm Rob." He clearly didn't recognize my name or who I was. He looked at my badge one more time and then silently decided something. I couldn't tell what he was thinking, but finally, he smiled and kept talking.

Even though he didn't know anything about me, my confidence allowed me to participate in the conversation, and we ended up becoming friends! It's not a lie to act the way you want to feel. It's not fake to show confidence you are still trying to gather. Don't let your lack of being where you want to be in this moment keep you from getting where you want to be in the future. Go make friends with A-level rock stars. If I can do it, you definitely can.

SUMMARY

- There is one thing you need in life to succeed: confidence.
- First, you need to know your stuff way before you hit the stage.
- Second, you need to put on a version of yourself that doesn't get freaked out under the spotlight. This is called a persona.
- I'm shy. Shy people can learn to go on stage and shred just like anyone else.
- When I'm nervous, I can remember that people like Mike C. believe in me. You can remember that I believe in you.

- Musicians and business owners alike use personas. This is nothing new.
- Confidence is built on a foundation made out of: what you say, who you know, and what influence you have.
- What you say is about that voice that lives in your head. This voice helps you understand who you are, but can also lie to get you to avoid things that make you uncomfortable even though those things aren't dangerous.
- If a goal can be set using the SMART framework, it's something you can accomplish no matter what that little voice says.
- Who you know is about the people you talk to. They don't just know your voice, you know theirs too.
- The internet makes it seem like friends who live close to you aren't super important, but that's not true. Likes and follows don't automatically make real relationships.
- The influence you have in life is about using your personal power to make choices. You can also use this influence to build others up or tear them down.
- Music can help you build your confidence. Use your musical instrument like a shield in your armor.
- Just because there are people in the music industry who still think all musicians should look a certain way doesn't mean you can't shred if you don't fit into their warped appearance bubble.

- You never have to leverage your sexuality or objectify yourself to prove that you belong in the musical world, just look at Sam.
- Music acts like armor that allows your confidence to manifest inside of you. This armor gives your subconscious self permission to let its guard down.
- Just because your voice tells you to bolt, it doesn't mean you have to, even if you aren't an A-level musician.

DISCUSSION QUESTIONS
1. What three pieces make up the foundation of your confidence?
2. What does Cory Churko say about making mistakes?
3. Is a persona a fake version of you? What is it?
4. How does music help you be more confident?
5. Why does your musical instrument work as a shield? Why does your persona work as rock-star armor?

ROB'S MUSIC NOTES

Now that you understand the truth about how awesome you are, let's talk about how building a rock-and-roll persona isn't you trying to be someone you aren't. This persona is built out of the things you already are that are difficult to maintain when going on stage.

No matter how confident a person is, when they go out on a platform where they have a spotlight shining down on them, they are going to feel nervous. It's just life. In the next chapter, we're going to talk about how to slay stage fright, but for now, it's time to learn how to put on that version of yourself who isn't afraid for when you hit the stage. The idea is to take the person you are when you're in a group of your most trusted friends, and get that person to show up when you perform. It sounds easy in theory, but in practice it can be complicated. That's why I want to show you my proven plan for creating and putting on your show-time persona. Let's do this!

GRAB A SHEET OF PAPER—I MEAN IT!

I know that this is a book, but I want you to actually go print out my persona worksheet at robsschoolofmusic. com/personaworksheet or grab a separate piece of paper because things are about to get real, and I really need you to write down this stuff. Make sure you don't leave anything blank. The more specific you are, the more this will help you.

1. When you are with the most supportive people in your life, how do you feel?

2. Why do you think being with them makes you feel this way?

3. Do you love and accept yourself the same way your best friends do?

4. If you were telling yourself that you aren't good enough or talented enough, what would your support team say to you? What would I—Rob—say to you to help you understand that you are awesome?

5. What do you want to name your persona?

It's important for you to memorize a script that you can use to build yourself up before you perform. We are going to make that script together, but first I want to model for you what my answers to these questions are and what my script looks like. I've been doing this for a long time, and I promise you it's worth the effort because it works!

Rob's Answers and Script

1. When you are with the most supportive people in your life, how do you feel?

I feel safe and loved. I feel adequate to any task. I feel relaxed, confident, and ready to take on the world. This is especially true if one of my people needs help. I will do anything I can to make sure they get the help they need, even if it's not from me.

2. Why do you think being with them makes you feel this way?

Because they have proven to me that I can trust them. They have supported me through all the things I have gone through in life so far. And when I'm feeling down, they remind me of all the things I've been able to accomplish through hard work. No, nothing came to me naturally, but I was able to learn how to do the things that are important to me, including music.

3. Do you love and accept yourself the same way your best friends do?

Sometimes I do. It can be hard for me to remember that I have worked to prepare myself to be able to go out on stage and rock, even after all these years. When I'm feeling too inside my head, I try to hear the voice of my dad cheering me on. I try to think about what Mike C. would say. Then I think about what James and Brian would tell me. When I channel their belief in me, it helps me believe in myself and pump myself up.

4. If you were telling yourself that you aren't good enough or talented enough, what would your support team say to you? What would I—Rob—say to you to help you understand that you are awesome?

They would remind me how hard I've worked and how many hours I've put in. They would tell me they believe in me. They would remind me this truth about life that Cory Churko said at the beginning of this chapter: "Sometimes you make mistakes, and that's okay. It's just human. Everybody makes mistakes. So you just have to be confident that you're going in as prepared as possible."

And what would I say to you, or to myself, in this case?

I would remind myself that no one ever picked up a guitar to have a bad time and that music is supposed to be fun. I would remind myself that I have bombed various times at different shows, but was able to turn things around. I would acknowledge the fact that feeling afraid happens even when we're not in danger, and that I don't have to let fear stop me from moving forward. I would also tell myself that the people who love me aren't going to stop loving me if I mess up, and that includes fans.

I would retell myself the story about how when Billie Eilish sang one of her brand new songs at a concert for the first time, she forgot some of the lyrics and her fans didn't care. They weren't upset. When she was disappointed on her performance, her fans comforted her and told her not to be so hard on herself.

Finally, I would tell myself that I have put in the hard work so that I can play my best, and at the end of the day, that has to be enough. Will I still make mistakes? Yes, definitely. But so do amazing musicians like Rod Castro and Rosh Roslin. In other professions every single day, other people make mistakes and they still keep going. I can too, and so can you.

5. What do you want to name your persona?

Rob the Rock Star

The Self-Given Pep Talk

Now that I have my answers all written down, I'm going to plug them into a formula to give myself a pep talk that I can use any time I need Rob the Rock Star to come alive. Then, you're going to use your answers to make your own pep talk to memorize.

The Formula

Listen, I know you might be a little freaked out about going on stage right now, but you don't need to be. You're [INSERT PERSONA NAME] and you've worked hard to get to where you are right now. You are stupid awesome at being you, and don't forget that.

If your best friends were here, you would feel [INSERT FEELINGS FROM YOUR ANSWER TO QUESTION 1] because they believe that you are [INSERT THINGS YOUR PEOPLE WOULD REMIND YOU OF FROM QUESTION 2].

Even if you don't feel that way right now, you can borrow the belief from your friends and from Rob when you're unsure about **[INSECURITIES THAT CAME UP IN YOUR ANSWER TO QUESTION 3]**.

I want you to remember that you are **[THINGS YOU GOT REMINDED OF IN YOUR ANSWERS TO QUESTION 4]** and that means you can do this.

You're **[INSERT PERSONA NAME]** and you've practiced super hard. You're ready to go out there and invite people to experience music with you. That's what they came here for. Believe! You've got this!

ADAPTING THIS SCRIPT

Before I show you what my script looks like, I want you to know that this script isn't just helpful when you're getting ready to go play music. You can adapt it and change it to fit any thing you're having a hard time with. Got a big test? Afraid to ask out the person you've had a crush on for the last six months? Adjust the script and pump yourself up!

Mindset is everything, and this short chunk of text will give your brain something to fill itself with when you banish the negativity that is trying to take up space in there.

ROB'S PEP TALK TEXT COMPLETED

Listen, I know you might be a little freaked out about going on stage right now, but you don't need to be. You're Rob the Rock Star and you've worked hard to get to where you are right now. You are stupid awesome at being you, and don't forget that.

If your best friends were here, you would feel safe, loved, and adequate for any task, you would also feel relaxed, confident, and ready to take on the world because they believe that you are able to get through tough things, work hard to learn what you don't know, and keep going.

Even if you don't feel that way right now, you can borrow the belief from your friends and from Rob when you're unsure about whether you're qualified to rock.

I want you to remember that you are here to have fun, when you make a mistake you can turn things around, the fans are there to cheer you on, and you've put in the hard work to prepare for this show and that means you can do this.

You're Rob the Rock Star and you've practiced super hard. You're ready to go out there and invite people to experience music with you. That's what they came here for. Believe! You've got this!

Print it, Text it, Memorize it

Now that you've seen an example of what you need to create based on your answers to the questions in the first part of this note, I want you to use the plug-and-play formula to write your own pep talk. Then you're going to take things one step further.

Put this thing everywhere. Type it up, print it out, and tape it up on the wall where you can see it every day. Text it to yourself and read it when you have some downtime or whenever you need to borrow some courage. Memorize it.

The goal is for you to know this pep talk so well that even when you're feeling stressed and other things slip out of your memory (stress does that), you can still remember this pep talk and give it to yourself. If you're alone, say it out loud in the mirror. If you're around a bunch of people and you don't want to say it in front of them, go take a quick bathroom break and whisper it to yourself in the privacy of a stall.

This might sound a bit extreme, but I promise that if you make this a habit, putting on your rock-star persona will become automatic and easy. That's what you want, right? This is the step you need to take so that you don't freeze in fear. Try it and let me know how you feel afterward, okay?

CHAPTER 7

Slaying Stage Fright - Before You Step On Stage

"I want everyone to know that many performers suffer from anxiety about performing in front of people—as cocky as some [of them may] seem. I was always nervous in front of a microphone if I had to speak in front of people when I was young and in school. It translated into kind of a shy disposition on stage. One story that helped was [in] Tony Bennet's biography [I was reading], and in the book he mentions stage fright. He told Frank Sinatra how he was feeling and Frank shared something like, 'That shows you care. You should be nervous and actually the crowd will accept that. Be yourself and be with the fact that you're really uncomfortable. You'll see that the crowd will kind of respond to you and you're going to get over it.'"

—Bruce Kulick (*Bruce played guitar with KISS from 1984 to 1996, and is currently the Grand Funk Railroad guitarist*)

Like teachers all over the world, I have a list of philosophies based on my past experiences that I love sharing with my students. My philosophy on stage fright has a lot to do with what we talked about in the last chapter. The truth is, if I can manage to fight off stage fright when I'm as shy as I am, then anyone can. Most people I work with don't usually believe that I'm shy because they are so used to me putting on my rock-star persona. But my shyness doesn't just go away.

THIS IS HOW SHY I AM, FOR REAL

When I was a kid, I would be afraid to approach the counter at the pizza shop, even though that was the only place to find all the gooey saucy goodness. Why? Because there was a person there that I would have to interact with, and that felt super scary to me. Sometimes it still does. I was so shy back then, that even at family events I would kind of hug the wall or make sure I was right next to my parents.

My dad and mom got me into martial arts when I was 9 to help me with my shyness. And yes, those lessons gave me confidence, but not in the traditional sense. I have always been a super loyal person, so knowing I could protect my sister, cousins, and friends was important to me. I have almost all girl cousins (except for one) and I have always been super protective of them and my sisters.

Martial arts gave me the confidence of knowing I could defend myself, but that didn't directly deal with my problem of feeling nervous about talking to people. This wasn't the same feeling I got when I started playing music seriously at 13, though. Karate was over at 16 because by then, music had taken over. My band was my team. I believed in them and they believed in me. We would defend each other and then go up on stage and show everyone what we could do. But that was with my team. In everyday life, I'm on my own a lot and that's totally different.

Now, it's my job to sit and talk to my students and staff all day, every day. Does that mean my shyness has disappeared? No way. It still pops up quite frequently. Students tell me that they would never guess I'm shy because that's not what they see. It's something that goes on behind the scenes in my mind constantly, though. So, if you're feeling that way, you aren't alone. I've just learned how to use my rock-star persona and one other tool to deal with it better.

When I started playing music and writing my own songs, I transformed into Rob the guitar player: Rob, the guy who is in a band and who interviews famous rock stars on YouTube. I've created this character, Rob the Rock Star: Rob from Rob's School of Music. It's my persona. This guy is loud and confident and remembers how much support he has and how hard he's worked to get to where he is. This works for me. At one point in my career, I even used a stage name to help me engage this mode of myself.

But even today, sometimes I go into a Starbucks

to order a drink and get shy. I have to remind myself "You're Rob from Rob's School of Music and you can absolutely order coffee!" I bring that persona with me everywhere I go.

In the last chapter, I taught you how to create your own persona. In this chapter, we're going to talk about the other way you can slay stage fright in addition to using your carefully crafted rock-star persona. The other key factor in fighting stage fright is to know your crap. I'm not kidding. You can know way before you ever get to the show whether you'll play well or not depending on how much preparation and practice you put in.

YOU HAVE TO PRACTICE

The truth is, if a gig is five days away, the gig has basically already happened even though it's in the future. What do I mean by that? If I haven't already done the work, nothing is going to change between now and then. Preparation is so important!

You know before you even start a show the quality of the work you've been bringing to the table at practice. Yes, nervous energy exists. But you always have the choice to take it and turn it into productive energy for your performance.

Yes, you should make sure you bring your A-game, but if you have the skills to back up the performance, you've already done the work. That's all you need.

Before my students have a show, I tell them, "Hey, it's already over." They look at me like I'm confused and say "What are you talking about, Rob?" I tell them "It's over. It's going to go by so quickly that we're going to be celebrating together in a minute. It's already gone and you've already achieved greatness and we're both sitting over there talking about how awesome it was. Now, go let everyone see that awesomeness on stage."

FAILURES COME FROM NOT BEING FULLY PREPARED

These days, Sam and I have a band together that writes original music, writes music placements for film and television, and often performs at corporate events. We're called heatedXchange because of how our music melds together passionately when we perform. Well, back in 2016, Sam and I decided to change from an acoustic duo to a full band. We put something up on Craigslist and social media, doing an open call for musicians. In that message, we assigned everyone four songs to learn to showcase the different styles we would need them to play.

I have always made sure to know my parts before I show up for any gig. Otherwise, what's the point? You know you won't play well. The ability to play a certain song isn't just going to magically manifest itself to your fingers without any practice involved. Let this paragraph serve as foreshadowing about what is coming next.

Over the course of two days, we were looking for a keyboard player, a bass player, and a drummer. Some of the people who showed up were 10, 15, 20 years older than me. I didn't care. But what I did care about was that they were playing with the same level of skill that they had probably been playing with since they were teenagers. That bummed me out. It bummed them out, too.

You could see it in their faces that they hadn't done their homework. They must have honestly thought that they could wing it. But that's not how you should approach music.

We already had an established duo that had done a ton of work. We weren't starting from nothing and we needed people to take the situation seriously. Some of the people who came to audition hadn't thought about that, and it showed.

It's sad when you see some of these musicians and how they plateau and refuse to push themselves to level up their skills. So when we gave them the material we needed them to be able to play, they couldn't manage any of the more complicated licks or riffs. They would simplify the songs to where they were comfortable. That zapped all the magic right out of the songs. I'm sure it won't surprise you when I tell you that we didn't pick any of the musicians who hadn't done the work to be part of our band. Learn from their mistakes.

Learning to Diversify

Different genres of music require different playing skills. If you want the versatility to be able to play in bands that perform more than just one genre of music, you have to be willing to learn different styles and skills. If you can learn those diverse skills and styles, then you will become a well-rounded musician. If you only know how to play AC/DC-Angus-Young licks all day long, you won't be able to play "Cake by the Ocean" by DNCE or "Look What You Made Me Do" by Taylor Swift.

If you want to be able to play whatever, you need to practice and work on songs that make you uncomfortable at first. That's part of becoming a musician with a skill that you can harness in any musical environment, no matter the genre. But what about when you get stuck before you start because you let social media get to you?

Social Media Musicians and Doctoring

I know I've been hinting toward this for the entire book so far, but it's time to address the elephant in the room. And this musical elephant is great at hiding behind technology and the fact that they don't have to play live gigs to get likes and follows. Now we're going to talk about social media musicians and doctoring.

Let me start this section off with a disclaimer: I am not saying that social media is all bad. If you know anything about me and my music school, you know that we have an epic YouTube channel where my students get to ask legends of the music world questions. These interviews serve as a way for my students to accelerate their music industry knowledge by tapping into the deep reserves of wisdom that my guests have.

The irony isn't lost on me that my guests, who are live on social media with me, usually bring up the fact that a lot of young musicians get discouraged by watching videos of performances that have been doctored. I know I already told you that when you watch something online and feel intimidated by what someone can do in that moment, you can choose intimidation or inspiration. That's true and I stand by that. But you also need to be aware that there are people on social media who don't care about being deceptive.

In my interview with Richard Fortus (from Guns 'N Roses), he brought up how people film something and then speed up the video to make it look like they can play three to ten times faster than what they can really perform. Music industry guys, gals, and nonbinary pals know about this phenomenon because they meet aspiring musicians all the time who say "Well, there's no way I'll ever play like that." We older musicians feel obligated to tell you that some of the stuff you're intimidated by is fake. The person you see on that video also probably won't ever be able to play like that.

You have the filter that helps you choose inspiration over intimidation, but now you need to add one layer into the filter and be able to ask yourself "Is this thing I'm watching even real?" If something is fake, you don't need to worry about being intimidated or inspired. The best way to deal with doctored videos is to ignore them. Cross them off your mental list because you don't need lies to inspire you. And you don't need to give liars views or ad revenue, right?

Now that you know how to add that layer of filtration into your musical mindset, there's still one question left to answer in this chapter. What if you're experiencing more than just the normal nervousness that comes from stage fright?

Dynamic Depression is Real

One of the things I have seen happen is that musicians confuse dynamic depression for stage fright. Stage fright is something you can work through by preparing. Depression doesn't work the same way. When you're feeling sad for prolonged periods of time, even when you aren't about to go on stage, it's time to seek professional help.

In Chapter 10, I'm going to go into more depth about mindset and mental health, but here I want you to understand that not all anxiety is created equally. You could be shy like me. But you could also be experiencing anxiety related to conditions like chronic depression, obsessive compulsive disorder, etc. I'm an expert in helping people shred. But there are also experts out there who know how to help you understand why you're feeling the way you do. If you have this knot of heavy feelings down in your gut and you keep thinking "Something is wrong," get outside help.

And now that we've gone over the ideas behind conquering stage fright, let's take a look at a practical tool you can use to make sure it doesn't get the best of you.

Summary

- If you're shy, that doesn't mean you can't go on stage.
- Martial arts helped me be confident about defending the people I love, but that didn't naturally transition into helping me be more confident about speaking to others or performing.
- My band was my support team, and that helped me. We believed in each other.
- My shyness didn't disappear, I just learned how to keep going in spite of it.
- Slaying stage fright is one part using your rock-star persona, one part intense preparation.
- Know your crap.
- Bring your A-game, but you also make sure you have the skills to back up the performance before you ever get there.

- If you don't prepare, you won't play well. Period.
- You should never approach music by thinking you can wing it.
- If you don't prepare, you won't be picked to join any band.
- If you only play the same kind of song, you won't be able to learn the skills you need to play different styles.
- If you want to be able to play whatever, you need to practice and work on songs that make you uncomfortable at first.
- Some videos you see on social media are doctored. They're fake. Ignore these liars. Don't give them more views or any ad revenue.
- There are times when what you are feeling might be more than stage fright. Depression is real and should be taken seriously.

DISCUSSION QUESTIONS

1. Does being shy or anxious disqualify you from shredding?
2. Besides your rock-and-roll persona, what other tool can you use to make sure you slay stage fright?
3. If you start practicing five days before your gig, will it go well?
4. Sometimes we might feel more than stage fright. What should you do if you're feeling depressed?

ROB'S MUSIC NOTES

In this music note, we're going to talk about how you can create a practical checklist you can use whenever you're getting ready for a live gig. As I mentioned in the last section of the book, you need to have a plan weeks out if you really want to be able to execute rocktastic playing at your performance.

YOUR PERSONA PEP TALK

The first thing you need on your list is a rundown of the mental preparation you need to do daily so that when you feel stress or anxiety related to performing, you can adjust quickly. In the last music note, we went over a proven way to create a pep talk that you can give yourself whenever you're feeling nervous. This is the first thing you need to have in your arsenal as you prepare for your gig.

You should be using this pep talk at least once daily by now. The best way to play an awesome show is to be prepared way before it ever happens. And one of the ways to do that is to make sure your mind is right. You are awesome, and you need your pep talk and your persona to help you live in that mindspace every day.

YOUR SET LIST AND MUSIC SHEETS

One of the things I don't go full in on when it comes to technology is digital music sheets. Yes, iPads and Surface Pros are great. I get why a lot of musicians use them. But when you're in prep mode, you need to be able to write notes on an actual piece of paper. Whether you're using tabs, chords, or sheet music, you need to print out the sheets for each song on your set list and commit to learning them.

What do I mean "learning them"? Whenever you get a new piece of music, you should go all the way through the piece to make sure you understand the different techniques and time signatures that the piece requires. If you need help, don't wait until later. Get your teacher or mentor in on this as soon as possible. Go through the music with them instead of alone if you haven't played a lot of gigs before.

The next step is to learn chunks of the song. Splitting up the music in sections will help you learn it more easily. If you sit down and try to learn the entire thing at once, you're probably going to suffer from information overwhelm. Don't worry about trying to play the entire thing all the way through, yet.

Once you learn each section well, start trying to play through the first two sections together. When you master that, add the next piece and so on until you can play through the entire song without having to stop and adjust your instrument or pause to flip through to the next page of music. The amount of time it takes you to learn a song will vary, but the more songs you learn to play, the faster this process will get.

When you can play the song through well without having to look at every note on your music sheet, it's time to practice with your band. The other members should have been going through the same process on their instruments. It's okay if you start off playing together and things don't connect instantly. That's why you practice. It's hard to blend everything together right away, especially if you're still getting used to playing with each other.

Next, make sure to go through this process for each song on your set list. This is why you need to plan way ahead of time, because in order to perform well, you need to go through this process for each and every song you plan to play. And you need both individual practice time, and time set aside for practicing it with your band.

Since we talked about the steps and you know what each piece is made of, I can introduce my Music Gig Prep Checklist that you can use whenever you're getting ready to go on stage. Using a repeatable process means you will be able to create repeatable results.

Music Gig Prep Checklist
(Check off each item as you complete it. You can also make mini checklists for each song if that helps you go through the process better.)

[ ] Step 1
Have your Persona Pep Talk memorized and start saying it to yourself each time you sit down to learn or practice your music.

[ ] Step 2
Decide on a set list with your bandmates.

[ ] Step 3
Get the different music you need for the songs on your set list printed out whether you're using tabs, chord sheets, or sheet music.

[ ] Step 4
Listen to those songs a lot whenever you aren't practicing. You want to get your brain used to the way they sound.

[ ] Step 5
Split each song into manageable sections and learn to play those sections individually.

[ ] Step 6
Start adding sections of the song together until you can play all the way through.

[ ] Step 7
Get together with your band to practice the song together.

[ ] Step 8

Do steps 3 through 7 for all the songs on your set list.

[ ] Step 9

Go rock out and kill it at your show!

[ ] Step 10

Celebrate by telling your teacher or mentor how everything went.

CHAPTER 8

All Together Now – Community Is Everything in Music

"Any time that you have the opportunity to share knowledge with young people, it's like the best. That's so special."

–Nick Perri *(Nick has played guitar, written songs, and produced for bands like The Underground Thieves, Silvertide, Mount Holly, and SINAI)*

The truth is, when I was a teenager learning how to make my guitar strings say what I wanted them to say, I didn't really think about owning my own music school. But along the way, as I shaped my career around rock and wanted to be at home more to be available to my son, Jack, teaching music became super appealing to me. You know, my son plays the keyboard and the violin, and it's thrilling to me that I get to be there to support him as he travels through his own musical journey. It's turned out to be a generational thing. My dad was into music, I got into it, and now my son loves it. But it hasn't just been in my family that music has influenced my relationships and community.

When I first started teaching, I knew that I wanted to be like Mike C. Not necessarily because he taught me martial arts, although that was awesome, but because he became one of my people. And martial arts also gave me my music support system in the faces of James and Brian. Now, the older I get, the more I'm able to add awesome people to my personal life and also the community my students are a part of: all through music. In this chapter, I want to help you understand how music is so much more than a hobby, it's a lifestyle. And one of the biggest reasons it is a lifestyle is because you will create quality friendships through music that will stay with you for the rest of your life. One big proof of that for me is my YouTube channel.

ROB'S SCHOOL OF MUSIC ON YOUTUBE

When I first started the YouTube channel for our school, it was a way to create a community feel for my students in an uncertain time. Because of COVID, we couldn't meet in person and talk at the school for an unknown amount of time. I didn't want my students to lose the connections they had to each other or our staff, so I decided to do something that would bring us all together while helping us level up our knowledge of rock and roll and also life in general.

The interviews did everything I was hoping they would do for my students and more, but what I wasn't expecting was how many personal relationships I would gain from the channel. Once I started going, more and more people were like, "Hey, let me connect you with this person. I think they would love to help out your students."

I would reach out to this musician I didn't know, we would do the show, become friends, and they would give me another person to connect to. Why did this happen? Because when you're open to learning from other people in the music community, they want to help! Like Nick Perri's quote at the beginning of this chapter says, "Any time that you have the opportunity to share knowledge....That's so special."

Musicians all over the world understand how important it is for young people to have this supportive community, because when we were all growing up and learning to rock, it was more difficult to feel that sense of support. Now that the internet is so popular, you can spend a couple hours a week watching the interviews on our school's YouTube channel or checking us out on Instagram, and you have the built-in confidence that comes from knowing you aren't alone: The struggles you face are ones that every musician faces. This knowledge is empowering.

But my realization of how powerful the music community could be didn't come from any social media. The story of that realization goes back to before social media was even a thing. When I was still a teenager, I learned that even people who aren't musicians will want to be part of your musical community if you invite them to be.

Black Roses Revisited

When I think back to our sold-out show at the Antrim Playhouse, I remember more than just the fact that we headlined our first rock show. The thing that really sticks out for me these days, now that I have more life experience, is the way the community embraced us.

There were people of every age who paid to come to our show. But the support didn't stop there. Remember all the businesses that sponsored us by paying for ads we put on T-shirts? Yeah, I'm pretty sure those weren't the world's best performing ads. So, why did they say yes? I can't be sure, but now that I have my own business, my guess is that they saw a bunch of young guys willing to hustle for their dream, and they wanted to support that.

There were also people who helped with concessions, merch sales, and everything else. When you have a vision of something that can bring people together, and you help others see that vision, you can do amazing things like sell out a playhouse that has never hosted a rock and roll show before. But the power isn't really in the music itself. Yes, music is powerful, but that's because it encourages human connection. And those connections can turn what some people consider a hobby into something the rest of us consider a lifestyle. Because we know the power of the community behind it.

When I think about my dad driving that beat-up U-haul truck to get us from show to show, I don't just think about the music we played, I think about how he showed up to be our community of one until we could engage with other people to grow that community. Maybe you're looking for a community to pour knowledge into and get knowledge out of, too. Well, let me be that one person, the first one to show up, until you can engage with other people to grow your community. I can also guarantee that if you join our music school, you'll be able to up those numbers quickly. We are all about supporting and encouraging each other at Rob's School of Music.

Now that I have Sam in my life, we've had a lot of musical community moments together through our band heatedXchange, and some of them have transformed into lifelong friendships.

THANKSGIVING IN THE CATSKILLS

In the 2010s, for four years straight, heatedXchange would perform in the Catskills, New York, at a resort called Honors Haven, which felt like a cruise ship that could take you back in time. It was a resort on this huge property. Back in the day, the Catskills were famous for hosting families over the holidays and during the summer, and this resort still has all the feels I imagine families had when they visited the Catskills way back when. The resort would always be beautiful in fall with all the trails and nature to see, the leaves turning gold and red as they kiss autumn goodbye in what some people call "the most beautiful fleeting."

We would go every year at Thanksgiving to perform as an acoustic duo. We were there working as a couple, but somehow, we would always meet one or two of the families and connect with them. We would finish performing, and then hang out with one of the families for the rest of the night. Through that little gig in the Catskills, we were able to build some pretty amazing relationships with people we wouldn't have otherwise met.

You know that I'm shy. I told you all about that in the last two chapters. But what I want you to realize is that music gave me this point of connection with strangers where the shield of musical confidence created a bond that transformed us from strangers into friends in a matter of minutes. This often turned into hours of sitting by a fire, telling each other stories: sharing the special moment of connection that music allowed us to create. Music breaks down barriers because it automatically gives people something to relate to each other about.

One time, Sam and I met this couple from New Hampshire that we still exchange Christmas cards with every year—Mario and Laurie Anne. We also met another family from Texas, and one that had traveled all the way to the Catskills from France. These are real friendships that have lasted the test of time, and they were all made because of music. But this wasn't the only place where we made lifelong friends with music as the foundation.

A GUY NAMED DANNE

One time, heatedXchange was playing at a venue in New York City in the winter and the stage was crazy cool. It was six feet off the ground with giant LED lights. Once we finished our set, we were sitting at the bar and this guy came up to talk to us. His question was oddly specific. He wanted to know if we knew any producers. We kind of thought, "I wonder if he's serious," because every so often, as musicians, you meet a person at a venue who is having a good time at the bar and trying to make themselves sound cool by sharing things that don't always turn out to be true. But we wanted to give our new friend the benefit of the doubt, and I'm so glad we did.

We learned that the man, who had a thick accent, was named Danne. As it turned out, he was a big producer himself from Sweden who was looking for people to collaborate with in the United States. He had done really well in a past Eurovision contest. If you don't already know, in Europe, there is this huge music contest every year where countries battle against each other on live TV, and it's broadcast to millions of people all over the world. Sometimes even countries like Australia compete as special guests.

Now, we write music with Danne for him and other artists. He has written a lot of songs that have gotten big in Asia. We're still close friends in addition to our working relationship. In fact, a few years ago he came to New York and stayed with us for Thanksgiving. We had a great time with him, sharing our American traditions. Later that weekend, we went back to the original bar we had met at and played music together. It was a beautiful moment created by music and friendship, where things had gone full circle.

Music Connects

Earlier in the book, I talked about how music is a language made out of math. Because of this, it has the power to connect people of all cultures because it's a secondary language that everyone can understand, even if we don't know exactly what the other person is saying. When you're thinking about how to build a community and—on a deeper level—a support team, don't discount the amazing connections music can help you create.

SUMMARY

- When you find your people, your life gets better. Music can help this happen.
- It's been amazing to connect with my son through music just like my dad connected with me through it.
- People in the music industry love connecting with each other to encourage young musicians and also share knowledge with them.
- When communities come together with music as the center, awesome relationships can be built.
- The shield of musical confidence can connect people to transform them from strangers into friends.
- You never know who you're going to meet because they are interested in music too. One of them might be a Eurovision star you end up working with and being friends with for life.
- Music is magical because it's a language that transcends culture and language. Because of that, it can bring you friendships you might not otherwise have found.

Discussion Questions

1. Is music a hobby or a lifestyle? If it's a lifestyle, what can it do for you?
2. What unexpected thing happened as a result of the school's YouTube channel and what did this reinforce to me about the music community?
3. What does it say about a person when they show up to support you, music-wise or otherwise?
4. How does music work to connect people who haven't met before?

Rob's Music Notes

Since this chapter is all about community and connection, it seems like the perfect place to help you be the best bandmate you can be. These rules also apply to relationships outside music to help you be a better overall friend, sibling, cousin, whatever. These are the rules I live and play by and I hope they will help you as you build out not just your band, but also your support team.

The Most Important Thing

I want you to know that the most important thing about being in a band isn't looking cool. It's being cool. And by being cool, I mean that you need to be cool to your bandmates. Not that you need to wear the latest Jordans or have the best guitar. So, how can you be cool? Simple. Be respectful. Be on time. Come prepared. Have fun. And now that you know those basics, let's break down these ideas into rules that will help you shred better and be an awesome bandmate.

Rule #1: Be Respectful

Don't play or noodle around when someone is talking. Pay attention to what they have to say. If you're in band meeting mode, respect your bandmates' time and try to keep things running as smoothly as possible. Keeping your volume in check is also part of being respectful. Does everyone want to hear your awesome guitar solo? Of course, but don't treat the entire event like one long solo. You need to make sure the different instruments in the band are being heard. You also need to remember that all the voices of the people in the band are just as important as yours. Compromise is essential in bandmate life. Listening is also important.

Rule #2: Be On Time

In rule #1, we talked about how you shouldn't waste your bandmates' time. Well, if you're late to practice, you are definitely going to do that. I was always taught that if you're only five minutes early, you're late. If rehearsal starts at 7:00 pm, that means you need to be set up and tuned up by 7:00 and ready to go. Not that you should show up at 7:00. When you show someone that you value their time, you cement your bond with them. Time is the only resource that we can never get more of. Once it's spent, it's gone forever.

Rule #3: Come Prepared

You should come as an individual band member, already knowing all your parts. Be prepared to play and have fun. Nothing kills the mood more than stopping a song because someone doesn't know the thing they are responsible to play individually. Band rehearsal is for everyone who has already learned their parts to start learning how to play those parts together as a band. Remember: you can't wing it. This is true for everything else in life as well. Learn to show up prepared for whatever, and people will notice and appreciate you.

CHAPTER 9

Borrowed Magic - The Collective Transformation of Shared Experience

"One time we were playing 'My Own Worst Enemy' by Lit, and 'Flagpole Sitta' by Harvey Danger and guys were coming off the train in suits, probably from trading on Wall Street. They started moshing around us. We were playing acoustic, but they didn't care. They entered into that moment with us."

–Rob Spampinato

One of the most polarizing subjects in the live music space is the concept of covering songs. Some artists will tell you that if you aren't popular for playing original music, you've sold out. Other artists are excited to play covers, and some even form cover bands that play a long set list of another musician's catalogue. So, whose idea is the right one? I think my answer might surprise you (unless you paid close attention to the title of this chapter). But before we can get to that, I need to explain what a cover is and what a cover band does.

Have you ever heard of a cover? It's musical terminology for when one band sings the song another band or solo artist created, played or sang first. It might surprise you to discover that a lot of songs that were made popular by one band, were first written and performed by a completely different band. For example, earlier in the book I mentioned the song "Cat's in the Cradle" as an example of awesome songwriting because it has an interesting storytelling element. But I also told you that if you've heard the song, you probably heard the Cat Stevens cover. It wasn't originally written or recorded by Cat Stevens, but his cover of Harry Chapin's original song is the best-known version.

If you Google "famous songs you didn't know were covers," you can find several long lists of songs we all love, but were made famous by artists who didn't write them or record them first. Examples include "Girls Just Want to Have Fun" which was covered by Cyndi Lauper but originally recorded by Robert Hazard, and "I Will Always Love You" which was covered by Whitney Houston but originally written and recorded by the queen of Dollywood, Dolly Parton.

One of the things Sam and I do in our band, heatedXchange, is perform cover songs at corporate events. I never feel like I'm selling out when we play songs we haven't written, even though we're also songwriting partners. What we're doing when we play covers at events is living on borrowed magic, and there are few things in life quite as satisfying. But what do I mean "borrowed magic"?

IMAGINE WITH ME

Music has a transformative feature that not many other types of art can create. Hearing a song you know, which was important to you at a particular time in your life, triggers not only those related memories from the past, but also the feelings associated with those memories. I want you to imagine with me what it feels like to perform an original song on stage for the first time.

You just wrote it and you're terrified. You'll be great because you practiced like crazy, and you're going to play like the awesome rock star you are. But no one in the audience is going to be able to sing along or riff the parts on their air guitar because they've never heard the song before. That's okay and that's part of building your music career, but if you want to have moments of connection with people when you're first starting out and no one knows your songs yet, you will need to build moments of borrowed magic into your show. How do you do that? By playing covers.

You can also use covers to do something for your

music career that takes a lot of pressure off your everyday living: you can create a cover band to play gigs a few times a week so that as you're building your fanbase and demand for your original work, you still have money to live off of. It's not selling out to make sure you have money to keep going, even if you aren't making that money from your own art, yet.

Different kinds of creatives do this, too. For example, a writer who is trying to build out their fiction fantasy empire might write marketing copy for companies to pay the bills while they build up to the seven books they will need to finally have their fiction turn a profit. Artists might create digital work for marketing campaigns or websites until they can create a demand for their paintings or drawings. Playing covers or being in a cover band is the musical equivalent of this, and it's absolutely nothing to be ashamed of. In fact, it can create some amazing moments that you can use as power-ups when you're feeling discouraged.

MAGICAL MOMENTS

One of the ways people naturally want to interact with music they love is to see it performed live. But for many reasons, sometimes it is impossible to see the original musicians perform that music. It could be that the band stopped touring years ago, or one of the band members has passed away. It could also be that in order to see your favorite band, you would have to spend at least $400 a ticket for horrible seats and your budget just won't allow for that right now. So, what is a music lover to do? That's right, go see a cover band. Why? Because that's the only solution that fulfills the fan's need for that specific type of live music.

Throughout the United States, at any given time, you can find all sorts of musicians who are touring as cover bands. Why do they do it? Well, because they love to play live to an audience, and they love to play that music too. Plus, they can earn enough money to live off of. The thing about covers that a lot of people will say is that if you perform covers, it must mean that your original stuff isn't good. That's not true!

When you play covers, it is to create a special bond between you and the audience that can't happen with your original songs until people take the time to learn them. And your audience members are much more likely to invest both money (to purchase or stream your music) and time (to learn the lyrics and melodies of your original music) if you decide to bond with them over music they already know first. Plus, playing covers can be mutually beneficial in another way.

When you play songs you love, it's fun. You get to mash up the strings to a tune you've listened to over and over. If you also sing, you get to belt out some of your favorite lyrics. And the audience, who probably has some specific memory associated with that song, will also get to enjoy singing along and entering into those feelings from some point in their past. It's a win-win. And it's a win you can use to make money while you also build your fanbase.

The moments you build based on playing covers also do something unique for your confidence. Yes, you'll be employing your rock-and-roll persona, but you also just need time on stage to help your brain understand that this experience is something you can replicate. When you experience the bond that happens between you and the audience when you play songs they know and love, it will help you keep going when you get to the difficult moments that music can sometimes bring. Let me give you a few examples from the cover-based portion of my playing career.

When you do a gig as a musician, there are a few moments that stand out over the course of thousands of performances. These moments create a magic that I can only describe with words as a musical high. And when I sat down to think about which moments I wanted to talk about in this book, I realized that a lot of them happened when I was playing covers with my band.

The first one I wanted to write about happened on New Year's Eve as we transitioned from 2019 to 2020. Sam and I were playing with heatedXchange in a 5-piece band at a ski resort. Holiday gigs can be super fun and also really lucrative. We were playing cover stuff, but it didn't matter because we were all enjoying the moment together. It really felt like the entire crowd, every person, was singing along to whatever songs we played.

In fact, we even made a huge mistake, and this moment still makes it into the top five of my list. How? Well, everything played out like this: Someone had requested "Ocean Avenue" by Yellowcard. We were glad to play it, but the drummer totally messed up the drums in the beginning so that we were all an entire beat off. Hey, it happens. Well, Sam couldn't really figure out a way to sing the song at that point because the band and the drums were not in sync. The only thing to do to salvage the song was to stop. That was literally the only thing that was going to fix it. But stopping is worse than making a mistake because the death of your momentum creates a vacuum of awkwardness that everyone watching can feel. So, we decided to switch to "Sugar, We're Goin Down" by Fall Out Boy. Why not lean into the humor of the situation, right? (If the joke is lost on you, feel free to look up the lyrics.)

How did the crowd respond? They went crazy! Everyone lost their minds and started singing along and dancing. The "Ocean Avenue" debacle was forgotten. And out of that mistake, one of my favorite performing moments was born. It was three minutes and fifty seconds of pure awesomeness that I never would have had if it hadn't been for a failed attempt at a different song and its one missing beat. Life is too short to dwell on mistakes. Move into it and exist there. That's the only way to approach music, and that's the only way I know to approach life.

The next moment I want to tell you about was at a county-wide fireworks show for the fourth of July. We were playing on a huge stage full of sound and lights. Every time we started a new song, everyone sang along. I could feel the connection between the audience and the band as if it was some sort of physical thing. We played "Can't Stop The Feeling!" by Justin Timberlake, and people were singing every word. We decided to go back and forth as a call and response. The crowd was so into it.

Everything mixed together: the lights, the sounds, the voices, the feeling that started in my chest and pumped out to my fingers as I strummed the guitar strings. Those are the kind of moments you don't forget, and you don't ever have to feel like those moments aren't yours just because you weren't the one who wrote the song.

BLack RoseS' performance at the Antrim is also on my list, but I'm sure you remember that story. It will live on in my heart as one of the best moments of my life. The final story I want to share with you is the one I mentioned at the beginning of this chapter, and the lesson it teaches is so important.

Sam and I had just started heatedXchange. You'll probably remember that at first, we were an acoustic duo—the full band didn't happen until later. Well, back in the beginning, one of the things we used to do together was busk. Busking is what happens when people perform music or other entertainment on public streets or places like parks for empty-hat money. For musicians, you can famously use your empty instrument case.

Sam and I were in New York City with our acoustic instruments, and we decided to play some punkesque-type songs. Well, as the train pulled up, we started playing "My Own Worst Enemy" by Lit, the acoustic version. Dudes in suits getting off the train—I like to imagine they had just come from a long day of trading at Wall Street—started to mosh! It was insane. When we finished that song, they were still going so we played "Flagpole Sitta" by Harvey Danger, and the moshing continued. It was such a bizarre moment in that it was both equally unexpected and awesome. I will never forget the feeling that Sam and I got at the metro station that day.

These moments are enough to help you remember why you're doing what you do as a musician. If you use these little moments like power-ups when you're down, you can maintain enough momentum to keep going. It's happened to me both while I was playing covers and original music, whether I was with Sam and our acoustic guitars or when I was playing with a full ensemble. The great thing about practicing these magical moments with covers, though, is that you will be less likely to be completely overwhelmed when someone connects with you because of one of your original pieces.

How These Moments Set You Up

When you learn how to live out these magical moments of connection between you and the audience based on someone else's musical genius, it will be a lot less overwhelming when someone tells you that what you've written has changed their life. The truth is, every moment in your life is building toward something else. And the moments you collect from cover songs or playing ten cover songs in a cover band are no different.

One of my biggest magical moments happened at The Chance Theater in Poughkeepsie, New York. I was there playing with my band In Question, and after the show, this woman came up to talk to me. She said, "Hey, you know your song 'Take On Everything'?" I nodded yes. "Well," she said, "my husband has those lyrics as the screensaver on his computer."

She told me the specific words that had resonated so much with him were "When I die, who will I be? Take on everything." It was a crazy moment! Something I had written was the thing her husband wanted to see every day. I can't even begin to tell you how magical that felt. It was one of those moments when I felt like, Hey, something that came out of my head is encouraging someone else! My words have power and they are helping people! That's an amazing feeling. I can't wait for you to have that kind of magical moment, too.

And if you practice having borrowed magic through covers, maybe you won't cry like a baby when this kind of original music moment happens to you. Maybe. No guarantees.

THE BIZ SIDE

Because I care about you as a business person, I need to add one more note to this chapter. A lot of artists and venues get confused about how to get permission to play covers, and I don't want that confusion for you.

It is always the responsibility of the venue to deal with the performing rights organizations like the American Society of Composers, Authors and Publishers (ASCAP) or Broadcast Music Inc. (BMI) when it comes to royalties. They are the ones who are obligated to handle it. In the different bands I've been in, we've had issues where venues hire bands and then get into trouble because they aren't paying their dues to their performing rights organizations. When this happens, the results are that those venues can no longer have live music.

There are dues that venues have to pay to stay in compliance with these organizations. But many venues either don't know or pretend not to know about them. Eventually, they always get caught. Large scale music venues know about this, but bars and restaurants that decide they want to have live music can often get caught by surprise.

I'm telling you all this so that you know taking care of these issues isn't a part of your job. But if you want to make sure your venue is complying with a performing rights organization, all you have to do is ask. As for recording a cover, that's an entirely different ballgame so make sure you get a professional to help you before you try to sell anything another artist owns.

SUMMARY

- It's not selling out if you play covers at gigs instead of all original music. Covers are a great place to start.
- A cover is what you call it when you play someone else's music.
- Just because a song was made famous by one artist, it doesn't mean it isn't still a cover. A good example of this is "I Will Always Love You," which was originally written and performed by Dolly Parton.
- Playing gigs with covers is a great way to be able to pay your bills while you build out your fanbase.
- Covers can provide an instant connection between you and your audience.
- Magical moments can happen from playing both covers and original music, but will come more from covers when you first start out.
- Covers give you the unique opportunity to connect

to someone based on a memory that evokes feelings related to hearing that song in the past.

- Bonding over covers will help you prepare for the day when someone connects with lyrics and music you've written.
- In the music business, the royalty-related responsibilities are assigned to the venue when it comes to you having permission to play covers.

DISCUSSION QUESTIONS

1. Why do some people think it's selling out to play covers at gigs? Is this true?
2. Why does it make sense to play covers?
3. How can you create magical moments with the crowd?
4. How will connecting with the crowd through cover songs prepare you for the day when your own words and music touch someone's life in a deep way?
5. Who is responsible for permissions and royalties for bands who play cover gigs?

ROB'S MUSIC NOTES

Have you ever watched Pixar's movie Soul? It's about a jazz musician who loves music so much that he tries to produce his own long string of magical moments. He's so focused on making it in the music industry that he misses the amazing moments in his everyday life as a music teacher. But one of the points of that movie (which I really agree with) is that you can't live your life waiting for the magical moments or trying to force them to happen. I feel like this is a mental block that a lot of creative people have.

The truth is, you can't manufacture these moments. You don't know when they are going to happen. The only way to get them, though, is to keep going. It's also important for you to enjoy all the in-between moments as well. Do I love feeling connected to the crowd? Yes, of course. But do I also love the everyday moments I have when it's just me and my son? Yes! I love him so much and I know that if I don't make my relationship with him a priority, I could get lost in chasing down music's magical moments.

So in this music note, I want to tell you that it's important not to try to force magical moments when you're feeling down. If you can't manage to power-up based on past moments anymore, it's time to talk to someone about how you're feeling: a friend, a fellow rocker, or a therapist. Music can't be your everything. It can't be my everything. You need to find balance and invest in what you say, the people you talk to, and the influence you have in life. And since that feels like the perfect transition for the final chapter in this book, let's talk about what mindset and self-care can do for you as a person and also as a musician.

CHAPTER 10

A Rest Is a Note - Mindset and Music

"I can't worry about the things I can't control. But what can I control? And I realized I can control a lot of the aspects of my own health and I just started looking into things I could do."
–Matt Halpern *(Matt is the amazing drummer of Periphery and has also worked in music education)*

When I first started making music, if you were a freak, punk rocker, and musician, you couldn't be an athlete. The dude running cross country just wasn't the lead singer of a punk band. Way back in the '90s, you had to choose which one thing you were going to be into. Honestly, that felt lame, because I was into a lot of things.

As a musician, I was into everything. I still am. I like jazz, the oldies station with songs from the '50s and '60s, heavy metal (obviously), rock and roll, indie rock, etc. And now, I have noticed that it's okay to like whatever combination of music you want. It feels like as we saw the rise of Limewire and Napster (the first serious music-sharing platforms), it was more and more okay to like varying music. And now that we have streaming options, people are way more open to listening to other bands and genres of music because they can listen to a band's entire history all at once. It's awesome.

And just like the idea of people being more into more than one kind of music has gotten popular, so has the idea of musicians getting into self-care. Now it's okay to be into fitness and emotional wellness. Now you hear people in the music world talking about meditating and journaling as they work on their mindsets. For a really cool glimpse into how and why these things matter to musicians, you should listen to the second interview I did with Periphery's Matt Halpern on the Rob's School of Music YouTube channel. We go so deep on what self-care means and how to figure out what routine works best for you.

These days, I take care of myself by eating healthily, exercising, and making sure I create a balance between my work life and my professional life. I'm a vegetarian in general and eat strictly vegan at home. My daily routine, even when I'm out on tour, is to be in bed by 1:00 am. I get up at 8:00 am. The first thing I do is get some sun on my skin. I walk, bike, or run around a lake near my house.

Self-care matters because if you're good to your physical and mental self, you can keep going. You need to be kind to yourself, and that is one of the things music can actually do for you: help you maintain a good self-care routine and practice self-empathy. Yes, you will hit notes that don't always work and mess up sometimes, but you need to be able to forgive yourself.

You already know about my lime green underwear and my David Lee Roth air-split. You also know that on New Year's Eve our band got an entire beat off during "Ocean Avenue" by Yellowcard and had to abandon that song completely. But life is too short to dwell on mistakes. Move into the next moment and exist there. That's the only way to approach both music and life, and I can prove it.

Making Each Moment Count

Like I said before, we only have a handful of moments that are really special in our lives. And if you're going to get into drugs or alcohol, you lose those moments. I know a lot of creative people feel things deeply, which means they also hurt deeply. But the answer isn't to try to cover up those feelings with a substance or by choosing to use your influence to tear others down. The best way to deal with strong, negative feelings is to work through them, create a great support group, and lean into healing practices like therapy and meditation even when things feel too hard. The last story in this book is a perfect example of that.

I worked with a student who reached out to me, and immediately I could see that she was in treatment. She looked like she was in chemo. Instead of dancing around the issue, she straight out told me that she had been fighting terminal brain cancer. She was hoping to make it to the end of the year.

She had already been through a really intense surgery where they had to remove one-fourth of her brain because of the cancer, and she felt like music would help her develop new pathways in her brain as it rebuilt itself. One of her goals was to learn to play the guitar. I didn't feel like I could charge her, so I told her to pay me with smiles. After that, we started jamming together and I started working with her as she learned to play the guitar.

As I'm finishing up this book, thankfully I have an update about my student. She was hoping to make it to Christmas of 2021, and she just stopped by at the beginning of February to say hello. Her cancer is in remission! The tumor has shrunk a little and she truly feels our musical time together is what caused that. She even started her own holistic business.

The gift of music gave her purpose. I remember that at one point she said to me, "Having music in my life makes me want to be here." That's what music does. And that's why I care so much about you and you being able to pursue your musical goals and dreams. It doesn't have to take something as traumatic as what my student went through for you to start moving forward on your musical journey. But it will require you to start being kind to yourself, and that means developing a system that helps you keep going when life is hard. But how? Keep reading to find out.

A Rest Is a Note

What does a good self-care routine look like? Well, that's sort of a trick question because there isn't one good answer: there are lots of great answers. Everyone is different and that means that a self-care plan that works wonderfully for me might not help you as much. For example, I know that I need seven hours of sleep a night and I don't feel great unless I exercise. As individualized as these routines go, though, it's not tricky to establish one that works for you. You really only need to figure out three main things.

Anytime you visit a therapist for the first time, they'll ask you about your self-care routine. They ask about it right away because it's vital. It can make or break all of the hard work you do in therapy as you work through your story. A self-care routine isn't anything fancy or complicated, it's just referring to three things.

First, are you getting good sleep? Second, are you eating healthy foods (eating junk all the time doesn't make you feel really great) and making time to exercise? Third, do you have a good support system of people who will encourage you as you make decisions to protect your personal boundaries and your mental health?

If you answered "no" to any of those questions, don't worry. You just need to make a few adjustments. I'm sure you noticed that when I talked about my routine, I mentioned how I eat, when I exercise, and how I sleep. But you also know that I have a support system in my parents, Brian, James, my son, and my girlfriend Sam. Plus all the rest of the cool people I work with at Rob's School of Music. But since we've been talking about music this entire time, I want you to think about a rest.

In music, there are moments when you don't play. These moments are marked with rest symbols and there are different symbols that tell you how long the rest is. When you feel like things just aren't going right in life and that your self-care routine isn't as robust as it should be, it's okay to use a rest. A rest is still a note. It's still a vital part of playing music. And when you're building out a self-care routine that will work for you, it's important for you to use the rest as you try to understand what works and what doesn't. It's okay to pause and reflect. That's part of life and that's also part of music.

You can always adjust your sleeping schedule and your habits leading up to bed time. You can always choose healthier foods to eat and create a better exercise routine for your schedule. And you can always find people to join your support team. In fact, a lot of the people on my team made their ways into my life through our shared love of music. Remember when I told you that my band was my first support system outside of my family and Mike C.? You can find the same thing.

I believe in you, and I know that as you test different things out, you can find a way to play through life with a routine that helps instead of hurts.

SUMMARY

- It used to be that if you were into one thing, you could only be into that. Now it's totally acceptable to have different interests.
- Musicians have gotten way more into self-care and mindset work.
- Self-care matters because if you're good to your physical and mental self, you can keep going.
- You will make mistakes, but if you forgive yourself you can keep moving forward.
- We only have a handful of moments that are really special in our lives.
- Music can help during the most difficult moments of your life.
- It's important to be able to balance out the different parts of your life: work, family, friendships, and music.

- Self-care boils down to a few things. Get good rest. Eat healthily. Exercise. And build a good support system around you.
- A rest is a note, and making sure you take time to rest is important.
- You can always improve your self-care routine, no matter where you're starting from.

DISCUSSION QUESTIONS

1. Do you have to pick only one thing, or can you like different things? What about genres of music?
2. Why does self-care matter?
3. What things make up a good self-care routine?
4. What areas of your self-care routine need to be adjusted?

ROB'S MUSIC NOTES

If you go through the following questions and answer them, you will get a clear idea of what adjustments you need to make to your self-care routine. You can write down the answers on a separate piece of paper or record them into your phone to listen to as you self-reflect. It's important for you to be honest with yourself as you answer these.

Your Self-Care Routine

Do you ever feel like there aren't enough hours in the day to complete all the tasks you have? Are you making time for quality sleep and exercise?

Are there people you talk to when you're feeling sad or discouraged? Do they seem to want to help you by validating your feelings, or do they just seem focused on fixing your problem so you can stop talking about it?

What is the quality of the food you're putting into your body? It's okay to splurge on your favorite pizza or ice cream cone once in a while, but do you find yourself eating fruits and vegetables regularly? If you often feel sick after you eat, have you ever thought of potential food sensitivities you might have? (You can work through this issue with a food sensitivity test and an elimination diet. If you need help, you can talk to a nutritionist.)

When you face new challenges in life, who do you have by your side? Is there a mentor or teacher around to offer you advice and encourage you?

Be honest with your answers and take a minute to run them through these filters:
Am I getting enough rest?
Am I managing my stress well?

How often do I work out?

Are there healthier food options I can integrate into my everyday diet that I still love?

Do I have at least three people I trust with sensitive issues in my life and am I also putting in effort to make them feel validated and supported?

In order to make the changes you need to your self-care routine, you can keep a journal. Write down when you feel awesome and when you feel down. Then write what you did that day in an effort to maintain good self-care. Every person is different so every self-care routine needs to be different. Figure out what works best for you and then try to be consistent. You've got this!

CHAPTER 11

Now What?

"I wasn't taught by schools. I was taught by 'trial by fire.' Jump in the lake and swim or you drown. If I had unhappy [guitar] customers, I was out of business."

–Paul Reed Smith (*Legendary founder and guitar maker over at PRS guitars*)

The truth is, I never really had a great time in school. I have a high IQ, but I would only focus my brain on things that mattered to me and English and math just didn't excite me. I would cut class to walk the hallways and write songs. Or, I would take a ride to the mall and buy a new CD. Then I would bring it back to school for people to listen to. The staff at the school told me I had ADD or ADHD. I skipped my SATs because I had a gig the night before. College wasn't even on my radar.

I was cutting so much class the principal told me I was about to get kicked out. I didn't care, and when I finally got kicked out, it was a relief. But the assistant principal must have understood my frustration, because he told me there was a community college that offered a GED and associate degree at the same time. So, I did that. It took me four years. Just at the end of that journey, something amazing happened.

During my final semester at school, I took a music class. I never would have thought studying music in college was an option. And once I understood it was, I felt like I wasn't good enough. But I did it anyway and I fell in love.

I decided to study music for my bachelor's degree and ended up at Ramapo College in New Jersey. When I first got there, I still didn't think I was good enough to pursue music, so I entered as a communications major. As part of my program, I took a music media class. It really helped me. That's when I decided to embrace classes like music business, music performance, and music production.

My education wasn't traditional in any way, but because I did things that were important to me, I was able to make a life I love. Everything I've done since then has gone back to that education. It makes me think of the Paul Reed Smith quote at the beginning of this chapter. No one way of education works for everyone. I learned a lot of things through trial by fire just like PRS did. But I also learned from structured classes.

If you know who you are and you have a goal in

your heart, it's so much easier to admit to yourself what you want to do with your life. That goal could drop on you at 7, 17, or 57. Don't ignore it. And don't be discouraged because of what you don't know yet.

The truth is, all people need if they want to learn an instrument with me is an instrument (I can give you specific recommendations on what to start with), wifi, and a computer. It's that simple. Don't let the unknown hold you back anymore. Take your hope and your goals and jump into whatever the next step is. For me, it was gaining more knowledge and experience, and that's why those are the things I offer to my students.

THE LAST NOTE

At the end of every book there has to be a conclusion, just like at the end of every epic album there has to be a final note. Now that we've come to the end, I need you to know that I don't like to leave my friends hanging. I consider you my friend now. You know some of my life's best and worst moments. You know how much I love what I do. And you probably remember how my music career didn't start off so great. Well, because of all those things combined, I work at my own music school to help people make their rock and roll dreams a reality. Have you ever wondered what you could do with the right teacher? With awesome accountability? With a mentor who cheers you on and pushes you a bit when you're ready to level up?

I want to be that person in your life. Or, I want one of our awesome music teachers to be that person for you if the two of you are a better fit for each other. Are you ready to take the next step in your musical career? Awesome. If I just described you, go ahead and check out what the next steps look like by visiting robsschoolofmusic.com/newstudent. And if that isn't you yet, that's cool too. I'm so glad you went on this journey with me. I hope you learned some cool things and can borrow my belief the next time you're wondering if you can slay stage fright. If you ever change your mind, I'm around, and I'm ready to rock with you.

Acknowledgements

Like any great band, multiple players had to come together to make this happen. There are far too many to acknowledge without me inadvertently leaving someone out, so I will do my best to start from the beginning and thank everyone who got me here.

I need to thank my parents, Judy and Al for their constant unwavering support of all my musical and entrepreneurial endeavors. Thank you for always believing in me. I love you guys.

I have to thank my sister, Jenny, for tolerating growing up with a rockstar in training during my teen years—and to her future husband, Guy, for taking good care of her.

Thank you to Uncle Ronnie, Aunt Mary, Uncle Gelo, and Aunt Karen for always coming to my local gigs.

Thank you to my martial arts instructor Mike and my guitar teacher Ryan for being role models and mentors who shaped me into the person I am today.

I have to thank my best friends James and Brian for being there for every major up-and-down in my life.

Brian, thank you for being an older brother, always there for advice and to hear out a crazy idea. James, thank you for introducing me to the guitar and being my musical counterpart for the last 25 years. I also need to acknowledge and thank Tom, Brendan, Drew, Jimmy, Tony, Gary, JP, Alex, and Eddie for rocking out with me, creating stories, and "living the life we were born to live".

I have to thank my son Jack for showing me I could love something more than music. I can't wait until we get to share the stage together!

Thank you, my beautiful Samantha, for being my musical and personal soulmate. There is nothing more special than being able to share studios and stages all around the country with you.

Thank you to every student and every person who's ever believed in me as a teacher, mentor, and friend. The gravity of that is never lost on me.

Lastly, thank you to my writing coach Kristin and my editor Maria. Without the two of you, this book would not have been possible.

About the Author

Rob Spampinato grew up the son of a talented drummer and after a false start with the guitar at five years old, renewed his passion for melting faces as a teenager in his first band BLacK RoseS. Since then, Rob has made music more than just a hobby—it's his lifestyle. By combining his profession with his passion, Rob has been able to tour the country multiple times, play in various bands, create and produce music with musicians all over the world, and start a music school that uses a custom approach to make sure no one else has the same false start he did. When Rob isn't teaching, touring, or writing music, he loves to spend time with his son Jack and his girlfriend and writing partner Samantha. Rob's favorite band is Pearl Jam and he loves traveling and the feeling of being out in nature.

CONNECT ONLINE:

robsschoolofmusic.com

robsschoolofmusic
@robsschoolofmusic
Robsschoolofmusic

Also Make Sure to Check Us Out on YouTube!

youtube.com/robsschoolofmusic